"Independent, Original and Progressive"

Celebrating 125 Years of UNT

Edited by Morgan Gieringer

University of North Texas Libraries

Denton

Published by

University of North Texas Libraries
1155 Union Circle #305190
Denton, TX 76203-5017

Published 2016

Printed in the United States of America

ISBN: 978-1-68040-004-5

DOI: http://dx.doi.org/10.12794/sps.125th-004-5

Cover design by Samantha Lawrence.
Photography by Joshua Sylve.
Image scanning by other UNT Libraries staff.
Typesetting by Bookworm Composition Services.

Contents

Keeping the History of UNT   **1**

Alvin Clark Owsley: Early Supporter of the Normal College   **5**

Annie Webb Blanton: Feminist Educator   **9**

A Nose for News: Student Publications   **13**

UNT's Early Social Clubs   **17**

Beulah Harriss and "Dad" Pender   **21**

The "Birds" Who Know No Defeat: The Story of Scrappy the Eagle   **25**

"Jazz was such a negative term in those days": The Early Days of the UNT Lab Bands   **29**

Julia Smith, Composer of "Glory to the Green"   **33**

O'Neil Ford and the North Texas Bandstand   **35**

A New Deal for North Texas   **39**

Pioneers of the Biological Sciences Program   **43**

North Texas and World War II: The Campus during Wartime   **47**

Raza at UNT   **51**

Fry Street: A Home Away from Home   **55**

Evolution of the Student Union   **59**

Desegregation in the Classroom and on the Football Field   **63**

Where the Mean Green Are Seen: From Fouts Field to Apogee Stadium   **67**

A Mammoth Find for Students   **71**

Unclaimed Jewels: Celebrating Old Maid's Day   **73**

Can You Dig It? Women Employees Can Wear Pant-Suits to Work   **77**

Literary Stars Were Once Students at North Texas   **81**

"Blow the Curtain Open": The Leon Breeden Years   **85**

The Third Time's a Charm: Becoming Known as UNT   **89**

Time Capsules Are a Blast from the Past   **93**

Merrill Ellis: Electronic Music Pioneer   **99**

Charles Dickens in Denton: The Vann Victorian Collection   **101**

The UNT Oral History Program   **105**

Stay Tuned to KNTU!   **109**

Groovy Students Attend the Texas International Pop Festival   **113**

LGBT Life: Living and Learning at UNT   **117**

Clubbing on Campus at the Rock Bottom Lounge   **121**

The Man Who Made the Accordion Cool   **123**

"Miracle on Ice" Inspires Hockey Club   **127**

The Mean, the Green, the . . . Armadillos?   **131**

Driving Into the Future   **135**

Acknowledgments

These stories from the history of the University of North Texas were researched and written by the following staff members of the UNT Libraries:

Emily Aparicio
Lisa Brown
Maristella Fuestle
Morgan Gieringer
Perri Hamilton
Marta Hoffman-Wodnicka
Sam Ivie
Courtney Jacobs
Julie Judkins
Robert Lay
Amanda Montgomery
Jessica Phillips

The UNT Libraries gratefully acknowledges the generous support of the UNT Office of the President toward the publication of this book.

Keeping the History of UNT

On September 16, 1890, a man dressed in a frock coat and top hat stood on the steps of the Denton County Courthouse and addressed the citizens of the city. This man, Joshua Crittenden Chilton, announced the opening of the Texas Normal College and Teachers Training Institute, the first of many names for the institution now known as the University of North Texas. The new educational institution started holding classes before a site for the campus had been chosen. After the speech, students were directed to a structure on the northwest corner of the square that would serve as the school site for the first year, with Chilton serving as the first president.

UNT's University Archive, established in 1975 by President Calvin Cleve "Jitter" Nolen, holds thousands of photographs, documents and artifacts that tell the story of UNT from its earliest days. As a part of the Special Collections department of the UNT Libraries, the University Archive is overseen by staff including archivists and librarians with expertise in preservation or rare and unique materials. Old yearbooks, student publications, course catalogs and unpublished materials such as scrapbooks, artifacts, faculty papers and campus photography line the shelves of the Special Collections vault on the fourth floor of Willis Library. These materials are kept secure because they are precious, rare and in many instances impossible to replace; most materials in the archive are only ever seen by visitors to the Judge Sarah T. Hughes Reading Room, also on the fourth floor of Willis Library.

In celebration on the 125th anniversary, the UNT Libraries have opened the vault to the University Archive th rough a massive digitization effort, special exhibits and publications showcasing the rich history of UNT. These efforts have brought the university's history to life: it's one thing to read about history but quite another to view it firsthand. An artifact like the original copy of President Chilton's speech on the courthouse steps, bearing fold marks from being fit into a man's suit pocket and written in meticulous cursive script, can transport the reader to another place and time. Looking at this important founding document, it is easy to imagine yourself standing on the courthouse lawn, the sound of horse-drawn carriages passing through the downtown square as President Chilton described the character of the new college as "independent, original and progressive."

Over the past 125 years, UNT has more than lived up to President Chilton's dream. Now the fifth-largest university in Texas, with an enrollment of over 37,000 students, UNT is still just as "independent, original and progressive" as it ever was. This book features stories about the people and events that helped to define the character and spirit of UNT. Each story is illustrated with photographs and artifacts specially chosen from the Special Collections department and the Music Library, both part of the UNT Libraries, whose staff are proud to share these wonderful memories with you.

up the question of advanced methods in teaching, and Normal schools and Normal Colleges have grown up all over the civilized world. Some under the patronage of the state or government, ~~and~~ others independent of either state or church, and to the latter ~~independent~~ class *Texas Normal College* belongs; its badge the ascendant star of Texas, and lamp of learning; in character, *independent*, *original* and *progressive*.

The scope of the college will include broad courses of study, with ~~the~~ abundant opportunity to students to elect or choose such studies as will best fit them for their prospective business or profession. Our aim will constantly be to

Page seven of the manuscript copy of President Joshua Crittenden Chilton's inaugural address, delivered September 18, 1890. Note the words underlined for emphasis: "independent, original and progressive." *From the Joshua C. Chilton Collection (UP0001).*

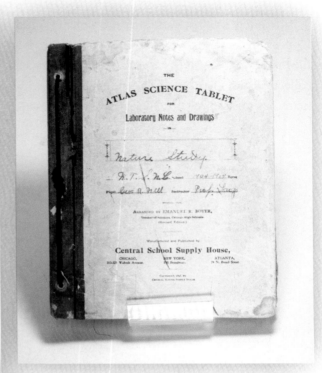

A laboratory notebook belonging to a student in the 1904–1905 school year. *From the Historical Collection (U0663).*

Class rings dating from 1901 (*left*), 1929 (*middle*) and circa 1900 (*right*). *From the Historical Collection (U0663).*

Students, faculty and members of the community are welcome to visit the Willis Library, where both Special Collections and the Music Library are located, to conduct research or simply to view special exhibits on display. Librarians and archivists are available to help you locate materials in our collections and assist in your research. Our collections are open to the public; however, advance notice is usually required for researchers in order to retrieve materials located off site. Please contact us if you are planning a visit. We hope to see you soon.

Morgan Gieringer
Head of Special Collections and University Archivist
University of North Texas Libraries

Men and women in a physics class, 1901. *From the University Photography Collection (U0458).*

Chilton, 1890–1893. *From the Joshua C. Chilton Collection (UP0001).*

A view of the North Texas State Normal College during the 1902–1903 school year. *From the University Photography Collection (U0458).*

Members of the spring Oratorical Contest, with Miss Blocker, a teacher of expression, 1902. *From the University Photography Collection (U0458).*

Alvin Clark Owsley

Early Supporter of the Normal College

Alvin Clark Owsley (1856–1938) played in integral role in the creation of the college that eventually became UNT and as an influential early citizen of Denton, helped to spur the development of the city.

Owsley was born in Missouri, the son of Henry and Louisa Mansfield Owsley. He received most of his schooling in California, graduating from St. Vincent's College in Los Angeles at the age of sixteen. He then moved back to Missouri to study law in the office of U.S. Sen. George Vest. Owsley moved to Denton in 1873 to work as a public school teacher. A year later he was the examiner of teachers for Denton County, remaining in that position until 1884. Meanwhile, Owsley continued with his career in law: he received his Texas law license in 1875, and by 1882 he was licensed to practice in the federal circuit and district courts for the Northern District of Texas.

Owsley married Sallie M. Blount, daughter of Judge J. M. Blount of Denton, on April 8, 1880. They raised a family in a new farm home they built on West Oak Street (then commonly known as Sand Street) in 1893. At the time it was constructed it was located outside the city limits of Denton, and today the area is known as the Owsley Addition and is home to a city park known as Owsley Park. Their farmland is now home to apartments and commercial establishments.

Owsley was a prominent member of the Denton community. He was the first president of the Denton Chamber of Commerce and a member of the Masonic Lodge, the Kiwanis Club and the Order of Knights of Pythias. In 1903 he served on a committee that was responsible for the College of Industrial Arts (now known as Texas Woman's University), also located in Denton, which opened its doors on that year. Furthermore, his career took him beyond Denton: he served three terms in the Texas legislature beginning in 1888, and he also served a term (1926–1928) as a district judge in the 16th District Court of Texas, hearing 473 criminal and 634 civil cases. Owsley was appointed special chief justice of the Texas Supreme Court in 1934.

In the 1880s Owsley owned the building on the corner of West Oak Street and North Elm Street. At the time it housed a saloon downstairs and his law offices upstairs. It burned down in 1884 and was replaced by a two-story brick building occupied by B. J. Wilson Hardware, which would serve as the site for the first classes of the Texas Normal College and Teachers Training Institute.

Owsley combined his interest in education with his service to the citizens of Denton when he was appointed to a committee to study Joshua C. Chilton's proposal to create a normal school. They recommended that the city

Alvin C. Owsley and Sally B. Owsley, date unknown. *From the Alvin Mansfield Owsley Collection (HM15).*

An image of the Owsley family home, built in 1893 on West Oak Street in Denton. At the time the family lived here, the street was commonly known as Sand Street. The land the family owned was eventually sold off and is now occupied by numerous apartments, but the area continues to be known as the Owsley Addition. Louise Street and Stella Street were named after the Owsley daughters. *From the Alvin Mansfield Owsley Collection (HM15).*

An early image of the Denton County Courthouse from the Owsley family photography collection. As a prominent lawyer in Denton, Owsley would have spent countless hours in this building. *Alvin Mansfield Owsley Collection (HM15).*

The Owsley children—Alvin Mansfield, Louise and Stella—in front of the family home. *From the Alvin Mansfield Owsley Collection (HM15).*

issue bonds, limited to $20,000, for the development of the school. Owsley was also named one of the first regents for the new normal school, serving as the board's secretary. Owsley was one of three Denton citizens appointed to act as local directors to assist the State Board of Education after an 1899 act of the Texas legislature placed UNT under the administration of that body.

Owsley died on April 27, 1938, and was buried in the Independent Order of Odd Fellows' cemetery in Denton.

The papers of Owsley's son, Alvin Mansfield Owsley, are held in the Special Collections department of the UNT Libraries. These papers contain several references to the son's childhood growing up Denton as well as documentation of his later career as a lawyer, diplomat and member of the American Legion.

NORTH TEXAS NORMAL COLLEGE

DENTON · TEXAS

DIPLOMA

This Certifies that NETTIE WILLIAMS, *has completed in a satisfactory manner the studies prescribed in the*

ENGLISH COURSE

of the above institution. We, therefore, by these presents, declare her entitled to whatever consideration

Scholarship, Industry and Moral Worth

are accustomed to receive.

In Testimony Whereof, Our signatures and the College Seal are hereunto affixed, this third day of June, A. D. 1897.

_____ *President of Faculty*
_____ *President Board of Trustees*
_____ *President Board of Regents*

_____ *Secretary of Faculty*
_____ *Secretary Board of Trustees*
_____ *Secretary Board of Regents*

This diploma from North Texas Normal College certifies that Nettie Williams completed all necessary coursework to achieve certification in English. The top of the document features an illustration of the Normal Building, and the bottom of the diploma is embossed with the NTNC seal. The certificate is signed by, among others, the Secretary of the Board of Regents Honorable Alvin Clark Owsley.

Annie Webb Blanton

Feminist Educator

When Annie Webb Blanton, an early 20th-century Texas feminist and educational reformer, moved to Denton in 1901 to join the faculty of North Texas State Normal College, the town had 4,000 residents. Over the next seventeen years Blanton witnessed Denton's population double in response to the opportunities afforded by North Texas State Normal College and the Girls Industrial College (now Texas Woman's University), the establishment of new businesses and the introduction of a railroad connection to Dallas and Fort Worth.

Before accepting a teaching position at North Texas State Normal College, Blanton spent seven years earning a bachelor of literature from the University of Texas at Austin while teaching full-time at a local elementary school. She graduated from UT in 1899 at the age of 29.

At the time of Blanton's tenure, Denton was still a prairie town. The first building on the North Texas campus, the Normal Building, featured a barbed wire fence around it to keep out livestock.

North Texas hired Blanton to teach English grammar and composition at the rank of associate professor. She taught five courses a semester and met with each course five times a week—the standard teaching load at North Texas at the time. Blanton also coached the North Texas debate team and helped establish both the *North Texas State Normal Journal* and the women's Current Literature Club. The 1908 the *Yucca yearbook* was dedicated to her "justice, impartiality, and interest in the students."

From the beginning of her professional teaching career, Blanton demonstrated an interest in contributing to the profession outside the classroom. She published her first book, Review Outline and Exercises in English Grammar, in 1903 while teaching at North Texas. Blanton would go on to publish three more books in her lifetime on the topics of grammar and education.

Blanton's time at North Texas was a catalyst for her future career. She learned the importance of participation in educational organizations from President Joel Sutton Kendall, a former state superintendent, and was encouraged to participate in the Texas State Teachers Association by Kendall's successor Dr. William Herschel Bruce. It was also at North Texas that Blanton established a close friendship with Emma Mitchell, a fellow North Texas teacher, who became Blanton's trusted advisor.

Blanton held many prominent positions throughout her lifetime. Fed up with women's second-class position within the Texas State Teachers Association, Blanton called for more opportunities for female members at the 1916

The faculty of the North Texas State Normal College, 1905, in a photo from the 1906 *Cotton-tail* yearbook. Annie Webb Blanton is in the upper right.

North Texas State Normal College students pass between the Main and Science buildings, 1914. *From the University Photography Collection (U0458).*

Student boarding houses across from the North Texas State Normal College campus. *From the Mike Cochran Collection (U0718).*

Postcard of North Texas State Normal College. *From the Mike Cochran Collection (U0718).*

TSTA annual meeting in Fort Worth. Blanton asked the assembled TSTA members, "How long are the functions of the women of the State Teachers' Association to be limited to paying a dollar to support its activities and to that of acting as audience and applause?" Following her speech, Blanton was nominated and chosen as the organization's president-elect, beginning her term in 1917 while still retaining her position at North Texas. During her year as TSTA president, Blanton battled sexism but was still able to pass constitutional revisions that made TSTA a more democratic organization.

In September 1918, Blanton resigned from North Texas and moved back to Austin after being elected Texas State Superintendent of Public Instruction. Blanton was not only the first person to hold the position but also the first woman elected to a statewide position in Texas. Blanton held the position of for four years, during which time she established a free textbook program, oversaw the revision of teacher certification laws, raised teachers' salaries statewide and took steps toward improving rural education.

After an unsuccessful bid for a seat in the US Congress, Blanton re-enrolled at the University of Texas at Austin, earning a master's degree in education in 1923 from UT and a Ph.D. from Cornell University in 1927. Blanton taught in the education department at UT from 1926 until her death in 1945, achieving the rank of full professor, only the third female faculty member to do so at UT.

Schools are named in Blanton's honor in Denton, Dallas, Odessa and Argyle, Texas. At UT a residence hall, originally for women only, is also named for her.

VIEW OF CAMPUS, HEATING PLANT IN DISTANCE, NORTH TEXAS STATE NORMAL COLLEGE. DENTON, TEXAS.

Campus of North Texas State Normal College. *From the Mike Cochran Collection (U0718).*

5125 Normal College, Denton, Tex.

The early campus of North Texas State Normal College looks rustic to us today with its dirt roads, low buildings and many trees. *From the Mike Cochran Collection (U0718).*

Cover of an issue of the *North Texas State Normal Journal.*

Staff of the *North Texas State Normal Journal,* 1908, in a photo from that year's *Yucca* yearbook.

A Nose for News

Student Publications

In November 1901, the first North Texas student publication, the *North Texas State Normal Journal*, was published. From 1901–1905, the *Normal Journal* served as the campus literary journal and student newspaper. Short stories, poems and literary criticism were published on a monthly basis alongside coverage of national and international news and updates on campus life. The final issue of the year, in May, featured class pictures and other features commonly associated with a college yearbook. In 1906 students voted to nix the May issue of the *Normal Journal* and instead publish all annual retrospective content in the University's first yearbook, the *Cotton-tail*.

Student yearbooks continued to be published under several different monikers. The *Yucca* followed the Cotton-tail and was published from 1907 to 1974. For a short four-year period (1977 to 1980) the yearbook was published under the title *Wings*, and from 1982 to 2007 the yearbook was known as the *Aerie*. The final yearbook was published in 2007.

According to James L. Rogers, author of *The Story of North Texas*, as the North Texas State Normal College reached "degree-granting status in the fall of 1916, the old *Normal Journal* seemed too much a relic of the precollege years, with its quaint mixture of news, stories, verse and homilies." The *Normal Journal* was discontinued, and its content was divided into two new publications: *Avesta*, a quarterly literary journal, and the *Campus Chat*, a weekly newspaper. The first issue of the *Campus Chat* arrived on October 25, 1916. The paper was initially a monthly publication but later became semi-weekly.

In 1970 the campus newspaper was renamed to its current name, the *North Texas Daily*. Currently the *NT Daily* is published four times a week, Tuesday through Friday, during the Spring and Fall semesters and once a week, on Thursdays, during the summer. The *NT Daily* is distributed free on campus with subscriptions available for alumni and other off-campus readers. Additional multimedia content is published on the newspaper's companion website, ntdaily.com.

Besides reporting on campus affairs, the student newspaper has covered national and international news events, such as the death of President John Kennedy. On November 22, 1963, the *Campus Chat* published a special issue on the breaking news coming from Dallas as well as the reaction on campus. The front page article stated, "From 12:45 to 1:30 the only students seen outside were running toward a radio. The construction crew on the new Union Building stopped its operation; the University Store was empty, with all the staff in the UB watching

Bill Moyers, onetime circulation manager for the *Campus Chat*, poses for a picture during his tenure as a North Texas student. *From the University Photography Collection (U0458).*

Campus Chat staff members look at page proofs, circa 1940s. *From the University Photography Collection (U0458).*

Campus Chat journalists Paul Recer and Carolyn Paine 1961. *From the University Photography Collection (U0458).*

The fall quarter 1924 issue of the *Avesta*.

Female students read an issue of the *Campus Chat* in their dorm room, 1942. *From the University Photography Collection (U0458).*

the television with many other North Texans." Students published a rare front-page editorial in this special issue decrying the assassination alongside a statement from university president J. C. Matthews.

Today, the NT Daily is completely written, edited and designed by students in exchange for course credit. Notable former student journalists at North Texas include journalist Mike Cochran (1957–1958), former Denton County State Representative Alonzo W. Jamison (1937–1938) and Regents Professor Roy Busby (1957–1958). Perhaps the best known is journalist Bill Moyers (1953–1954), who served as White House press secretary and as a news commentator and producer known for investigative journalism.

The Special Collections department of the UNT Libraries holds a rich trove of thousands of photographs created for use in student publications. While some were selected for publication, most others were never seen by the public until recent work by archivists to digitize these and make them available online and in this book. In the UNT Digital Library, the University Photography Collection includes over 6,000 digital images, with more added on a regular basis.

The Special Collections department also holds 50 issues of the North Texas State Normal Journal, *and 1,876 issues of the* Campus Chat *and 2,063 issues of the* North Texas Daily *are available to read online in the Portal to Texas History, a gateway to Texas history materials hosted by the UNT Libraries.*

North Texas Daily staff review the layout of an upcoming issue, 2013. *From the Junebug Clark University Photo Collection (AR0814).*

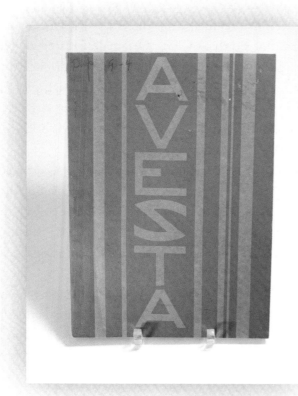

The summer quarter 1930 issue of the *Avesta*.

The 1906 edition of the *Cotton-Tail*.

UNT's Early Social Clubs

UNT has been home to a rich and vibrant Greek-letter community since 1952, with members making a significant impact in areas such as community service and academic excellence. Currently, UNT supports over 40 fraternities and sororities under four councils, but even before 1952, UNT students organized and gathered in various social and academic clubs and societies, usually segregated by gender.

At the turn of the 20th century, an energetic group of North Texas students gathered in the chapel to organize the school's first society. Unable to agree on the proposed constitution, the school's first society quickly split into two separate groups: the Kendall-Bruce Literacy Society (known affectionately as "the K-B") and the McKinley Society. After a few name changes and a trial co-ed integration, the McKinley Society disbanded. In 1902 the Reagan Literary Society was formed, regularly engaging in debates against the K-B, and the two rival groups met for a joint session in 1907 to form the Oratorical Association of the North Texas State Normal College.

While these groups were initially for men only, women weren't excluded from these activities for long. The Mary Arden Club was organized in 1902 under the supervision of Edith L. Clark. Originally created as a literary club for women and devoted to the study of Shakespeare, the club also provided its members various training opportunities through work and social activities. In 1922 the members raised enough money through pledges to build the Mary Arden Lodge, described as being "ideally located just east of the library." The Mary Arden Club remained active until 1970, regularly hosting teas, socials and literary lectures on campus. The records of the organization are now held in the Special Collections department of the UNT Libraries.

While the Mary Arden Club thrived, men's literary societies dwindled but were quickly replaced by social organizations. The first group to claim the name "Talons," a social club advertised as a "college spirit" group, formed in 1927; their mission was to "bring about a closer fellowship among the boys, to arouse a stronger college spirit, and to support all college activities." These early Talons coined the slogan "More Pep on Fewer Acres." In addition to attending all home athletic events and one away game per season, the group hosted annual jubilee programs and sponsored freshman students in a little brother program.

This early Talons club was followed by the creation of the Geezles and Pi Phi Pi in 1930. One of the most important events held by the Geezles was their annual banquet, noted in 1930 as being the "only occasion where girls are present at a Geezles affair." Rumor has it there was little love between the various male-only social groups. In the 1931 *Yucca* yearbook, a tongue-in-cheek version the Talons' constitution instructs that "no Talon shall go with another Talon's girl . . . pick on the Geezles' and the Pi Phi's," and "a Talon may associate with the Geezles at his own risk."

The Geezles hosted an annual ball, reported to be the only Geezles event that women were allowed to attend. *From the University Photography Collection (U0458).*

The Geezles were formed in 1930 to promote friendship on campus. This portrait of the 1942 Geezles members was taken outside the Administration Building. *From the University Photography Collection (U0458).*

The first student group that adopted the name "The Talons" was a men's service organization that fostered spirit on campus. They were responsible for the care and transportation of Scrappy the Eagle, the North Texas mascot, who lived at the Fort Worth Zoo. This photo is from the 1961 *Yucca* yearbook.

Members of the Kendell-Bruce Literary Society during the 1906–07 school year as shown in the 1907 *Yucca* yearbook.

The Geezles are no longer an active social club on campus, having disbanded in 1970, but past members still meet, boasting an active membership including past coaches, professional athletes, UNT regents and other prominent Denton community leaders. In 2012, those alumni raised over $200,000 to install "Spiriki," the large bronze eagle bust that sits at the player's entrance to UNT's new Apogee Stadium. The group also supports an endowed scholarship in their name.

Today's official student spirit organization known as the Talons wasn't formed until the summer of 1960. Their goal was to foster school pride and tradition by practice and observation. The initial group selected members based on an "interest in [the school], leadership, ability, character, and personality." In order to ensure no single Greek-letter organization could dominate the club and its interests, no more than three members of the same organization could join the Talons. The group's first members were charged with the care and transportation of Scrappy, the North Texas Mascot, who lived at the Fort Worth Zoo but visited campus for football games and the now-annual bonfire.

The University of North Texas owes much to these early social groups.

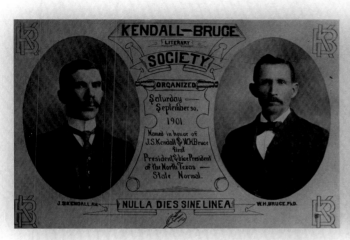

Advertisement for the Kendall-Bruce Literary Society featuring portraits of President J. S. Kendall and Vice President William Herschel Bruce. *From the University Photography Collection (U0458).*

Photo postcard of the Mary Arden Lodge. *From the Mike Cochran Collection (U0718).*

A co-ed group of students lounge in the Mary Arden Lodge, 1942. *From the University Photography Collection (U0458).*

Members of the Mary Arden Club, the first social group for women at North Texas, gather in formal attire in the Mary Arden Lodge, 1942. *From the University Photography Collection (U0458).*

Beulah Harriss and "Dad" Pender

Beulah Harriss and J. W. "Dad" Pender laid the groundwork for today's athletics programs at UNT but are known today for their contributions to academics and campus life as well.

Harriss moved from Nebraska to Texas to join the faculty of the North Texas State Normal College in 1914. She was the first woman hired as a member of the athletic faculty and taught both men's and women's physical education classes. Harriss supervised the women's athletic program and coached women's basketball. The women's team played three undefeated seasons between 1918 and 1920, going on to be recognized as state champions.

Harriss founded the Green Jackets Club in 1925 as a service and spirit organization and served as faculty advisor for this club for four decades. In its early years, members of the Green Jackets were drawn from other campus organizations; two women were selected to represent each campus club. Members attended every football game, provided help in blood drives and assisted at registration and other events. The organization was originally only open to women, but today's Green Jackets have both men and women as members.

Harriss was active in the community as well. Along with Della Marie Clark, she founded the Denton Girl Scouts in 1919, and she was a charter member of the Texas State Physical Education Association (now known as the Texas Association for Health, Physical Education, Recreation and Dance). She also organized the Texas Women's Athletic Association. Additionally, Harriss was one of 13 professors from UNT who started the Denton County Teachers Federal Credit Union (now DATCU Credit Union) in 1936. In 1976, the credit union held the first Beulah Harriss Day, in honor of the organization's 40th anniversary.

Harriss taught at UNT for 46 years before retiring in 1960. She died in 1977 at the age of 88. In 2015 Harriss was honored with a historical marker in the Quakertown Park, an effort organized and researched by Elise Clements as part of her work to earn a Girl Scout Silver Award.

A native of Gilmer, Texas, Joseph William "Dad" Pender came to UNT from Paris, Texas. His association with North Texas started when he volunteered to coach the baseball team in the summer of 1912. In the fall of 1913, President Bruce named him to the full time faculty, on which he served for 34 years, during which time he founded the government (political science) department. In 1925, he was named as the head of the Government Department and served in that position until his retirement in 1946. Pender also served as director of athletics and directed the band from 1915 to 1921.

Pender is credited with the establishment of intercollegiate athletics at the university. Pender and the student athletes cleared a briar-filled pasture for the first football field, located on what is now the library

Beulah Harris and the Green Jackets lend their support to the football team, 1926. From the University Photography Collection (U0458).

A women's basketball game on a court located next to the Library, now known as Curry Hall. The women wore bloomers in physical education classes and for team events. From the University Photography Collection (U0458).

J. W. "Dad" Pender in his office in the Manual Arts Building. The building stood on the east side of Avenue B across from the south end of Marquis Hall, roughly where the General Academic Building is located today. From the University Photography Collection (U0458).

Baseball team, c. 1913. From the University Photography Collection (U0458).

mall. He coached not only baseball but also football, track and tennis. In 1920, he organized the first Athletic Council at UNT.

"Dad" Pender was a lifetime member of the Texas State Teachers Association. He was a member of Pi Gamma Mu, a social-science honor society; the American Political Science Association; the Kiwanis Club; and the Denton Chamber of Commerce.

Joseph William Pender died in 1969 at the age of 93. The Special Collections department of the UNT Libraries holds a small collection of Pender's letters and photographs as part of the University Archive.

Bloomers were worn by female students during their physical education classes and by the women's basketball teams from approximately 1902 to 1912. During that time, women did not compete with teams from other schools but instead played against each other. From the University Artifacts Collection (U0493).

Photograph of Harriss with the women's basketball team in the 1920s. The photograph is part of Harriss' personal scrapbook From the Green Jackets Collection (U0449).

An eagle pendant presented to Roy Whisenhunt in 1924. From the University Artifacts Collection (U0493).

Vest worn by a Green Jackets member in the 1920s. From the Green Jackets Collection (U0449).

Vest worn by a Green Jackets member in the 1920s. From the Green Jackets Collection (U0449).

Vest worn by a Green Jackets member in the 1920s. From the Green Jackets Collection (U0449).

The "Birds" Who Know No Defeat

The Story of Scrappy the Eagle

In its first twenty-two years, North Texas operated without a mascot; the students were simply called the "Normalites." During this time, however, the college's administration was preparing to drop "Normal" from the name. With the name change in process, the administration also recognized a need for a mascot as voiced by the student body in a circulated petition in the fall of 1921.

A mascot was selected to promote a unified identity among the college's students and athletes. Most of the athletic clubs on campus were named the "Normal Boys" or the "Normal Girls," except for a few rebellious women's basketball clubs who named themselves: the "Dandy Doers," "Haughty Hits," "Limber Lassies," "Militants," and "Suffragettes" dribbled their way to glory on old dirt courts with their self-appointed monikers.

The mascot vote was held in January 1922, with students choosing between four animals believed encompassed the college's character: the lion, hawk, eagle and dragon. The eagle was chosen with 17 more votes than the runner-up, the dragons.

The 1922 *Yucca* yearbook includes a statement on the mascot selection by the editor, who draws a comparison between the growth of the college, from humble beginnings to educational prominence, and an eagle's flight, from valley to mountain top. The choice was solidified in 1924, when the U.S. Copyright Office registered the mascot's image—a majestic North American eagle, wingspan on full display, perched on a wooden branch carved with the inscription "Eagles"—which would be used in class pins, on rings, on athlete's letters and in collegiate publications.

After World War II, North Texas began using a live mascot trained by students at athletic events to boost school spirit—and to scare the living daylights out of the competition! The first, from Denton businessman Tommy Laney in 1950, was believed to be a South American golden eagle but was actually a South American fish hawk. Three students won a contest to name the bird, choosing "Scrappy." Scrappy retired to the Forest Park Zoo in Fort Worth in 1952.

Scrappy was succeeded that year by Victor, who unexpectedly died of heat exhaustion prior to his debut. Scrappy then returned as mascot, making scheduled appearances, until his death in 1959. In 1960, Victor II was appointed mascot for North Texas. Though this eagle was perfect for school spirit, the fees charged for his presence at games were too expensive, and he was returned to his habitat in 1961.

Eppy, circa 1980s. *From the University Photography Collection (U0458).*

The North Texas mascot riling up the crowd in a Mean Green convertible, circa 1979. *From the University Photography Collection (U0458).*

Winners of the naming contest for the eagle mascot: C. Richard Belt (*left*), Thomas J. Phillips (*center*) and Lonnie Renfro (*right*), 1950. *From the University Photography Collection (U0458).*

The year 1962 saw a new Scrappy pressed into service, but sadly he perished before making his first appearance. As the North Texas community mourned the death of the latest Scrappy, marching and concert band director Maurice McAdow decided to construct a papier-mâché eagle in an art class as an homage to the fallen eagle. The McAdow eagle was used at football games until the Talons purchased two serpent eagles in 1967. The Talons named the eagles Scrappy II and Scrappy III, and they were used for two years.

In 1969, the Talons elected the first human mascot, one of their own members, Larry Burrows, who was known as simply as the Eagle. From 1971 to 1973, the mascot's name was changed back to Scrappy, with another Talons member donning the iconic suit. The name change was short-lived, and in 1973 it was decided that the mascot would be called the North Texas Eagle, or simply the Eagle.

For a solid decade, the human mascot was known as either the Mean Green Eagle or the Eagle mascot. Then, in 1983, the Eagle was re-named "Eppy" by the Talons. Eppy remained in use until the mid-nineties, when Scrappy came back into use, continuing to this day.

Scrappy, circa 1950. *From the University Photography Collection (U0458).*

Scrappy greeting young North Texas fans, circa 1990s. *From the University Photography Collection (U0458).*

Victor, circa 1960. *From the University Photography Collection (U0458).*

"Jazz was such a negative term in those days"

The Early Days of the UNT Lab Bands

It's impossible to imagine UNT today without its program for jazz studies; the two are all but synonymous. In the 1920s, however, the forerunner to this program at North Texas was formed somewhat out of necessity, as an ensemble to accompany silent films, and starting in 1927, to support a Saturday-night stage show, which became a local institution in a prairie college town not otherwise known for its night life. The stage band, under the directorship of Floyd Graham—or "'Fessor Graham"—became known as the Aces of Collegeland. Numerous performers who appeared with the group went on to considerable success, including Louise Tobin, Moon Maids (who later joined Vaughn Monroe's band), Jimmy Giuffre and Pat Boone.

The participation of student arrangers in the activities of the Aces of Collegeland gradually generated an interest in—and a need for—qualified training in stage-band work. There were not many students qualified to arrange music, but an alto saxophonist named Gene Hall, from Whitewright, Texas, advanced to the point where he was arranging for both 'Fessor's band and the marching band.

Hall finished a bachelor's with a dual major in music and education in 1941. Expecting to be drafted, he began graduate studies at North Texas. Years later, he recounted:

> I come back to North Texas, and [Dean Wilfred] Bain gives me a graduate assistantship. I have three chores. One of them seems ridiculous now. One of the things I had to do was patrol the practice room area at certain times to be sure no one was practicing or playing jazz or popular music.

But Dean Bain ultimately had other ideas. When Hall approached Bain to propose a thesis topic, Bain told him he already had one picked out for him: to write a method book for teaching jazz on the college level. Hall finished his thesis in 1944 while working variously as a band director, a touring musician and a shoe salesman. In 1944, he replaced Don Gillis as staff arranger at radio station WBAP in Fort Worth.

In 1947, just as Hall was about to move to New York to begin doctoral studies and work with Don Gillis (UNT's first M.M. in composition), Bain's successor as dean of the School of Music, Walter Hodgson, offered him a faculty appointment to take over the still incipient jazz-studies program at North Texas. Through careful diplomacy, Hall obtained approval from the curriculum committee for a "dance band" program because, in his words, "jazz was such a negative term in those days." The ensemble's name, "Laboratory Dance Band," is the origin of the

'Fessor Floyd Graham directs "St. Louis Blues," 1942. Future director Gene Hall is seated second from the left in the saxophone section (the front row). *From the University Photography Collection (U0458).*

Graham teaching a class, undated. *From the University Photography Collection (U0458).*

Graham plays the violin in a classroom in October 1961. *From the University Photography Collection (U0458).*

Hall is interviewed by a reporter from WFAA-TV Channel 8. *From the Jazz Studies Collection (045).*

famous "lab bands" we know today. Even with the euphemistic name, jazz studies met predictable resistance at North Texas. In an oral history, Gene Hall recalled:

> *Generally, they [the music faculty] were antagonistic toward it. There were two or three who were very much in favor of it: Bob Rogers, a piano player, and Frank Mainous, one of the theory teachers. There were two or three who were very much in favor of it because they had played professionally, and they knew what it took to get along in the world . . .*

One colleague, while making clear that he had no personal animosity toward Hall but that he simply did not believe jazz belonged in the university, took his concerns to President W. Joseph McConnell. Hall described the outcome, quoting the other faculty member:

> *I told the president . . . Y'know, I've just come back from a national meeting, and every time I introduced myself as being from North Texas, the reaction is, 'Oh, that's where you have the jazz program! Tell me about it!' And then I have to go to the trouble of telling them we also have an orchestra, and an opera, and all these other things that make the School of Music. And the president says, 'Well, if you'd get off your ass and do something, you wouldn't have to do that, would you?'*

In an oral history, Walter Hodgson, then dean of the School of Music, explained that President McConnell had taken a keen interest in academic jazz, asking: "Hodgson, how is it that you have a course on music in the Middle Ages, you have a course on music in the Renaissance, Baroque music, music of the Classical era, Romantic music, contemporary [classical] music, but you don't have any at all that deals primarily with that one segment of music for which America is most famous: jazz!"

Others in the School of Music continued to hound Dr. Hodgson after the establishment of the jazz program, until he called a meeting of all music students and faculty in response to the uproar. Hall had no idea what to expect from the meeting, but Hodgson told his faculty, as quoted by Hall: "Ladies and gentlemen, we have a music department here, and part of our job is to teach music for a variety of purposes and a variety of people."

According to Hall, Hodgson cited the uniquely American nature of jazz and maintained that it was "part of North Texas' obligation to prepare people in this field." Hodgson finished, "I want you to know—all of you—that this program is here to stay. There's no use in you wearing out my carpet coming into my office and complaining about it."

The papers of Hall, Gillis and many other musicians with ties to North Texas are how held by the Music Library at the UNT Libraries, and an oral history by Hall is in the collection of the UNT Oral History Program.

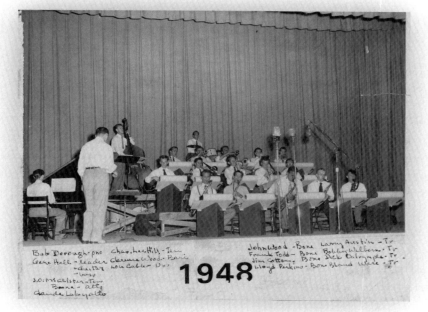

The Laboratory Dance Band, directed by Hall, 1948. *From the Jazz Studies Collection* (045).

The Laboratory Dance Band, directed by Hall, 1948. *From the Jazz Studies Collection* (045).

Julia Smith, Composer of "Glory to the Green"

You may hear her work every day and not even know it: Julia Smith composed UNT's alma mater, "Glory to the Green," which rings out from McConnell Tower on the Hurley Administration Building every day at noon.

Verifying the circumstances of Smith's birth took considerable effort by many members of the UNT Music Library staff, as contradictory information about her date and place of birth had her born variously on January 5, 15, or 25, in 1905 or 1911, in Denton, or in the mysterious locale of "Carwell," Texas. The fact that 1905 was her year of birth was generally a settled issue since the early 2000s, but in late 2015 electronic access to her birth certificate revealed that she had been born in Caldwell, Texas, on January 25, 1905, though the family gave a home address on Mulberry Street in Denton.

Young Julia Smith took piano lessons with Mary Anderson, a graduate of the Royal Conservatory of Music in Leipzig, Germany, and an instructor at North Texas. In her teens, Smith studied with Harold von Mickwitz at St. Mary's Institute of Musical Art in Dallas. Her father, James Willis Smith, was a professor of mathematics at North Texas and an amateur musician. Smith herself graduated from North Texas with a B.A. in English, remaining active as a musician during her undergraduate years.

She earned a master's degree from New York University in 1933 and continued her studies in piano, composition and orchestration at the Juilliard School of Music, studying under Carl Friedberg and Virgil Thomson, among others. She credited Friedberg with advising her that "the woods are full of good pianists," but "there are few really good American composers."

She served as pianist for the all-women's ensemble Orchestrette Classique of New York and took on ambitious composition projects, including her first opera, *Cynthia Parker*. She intended for that work to coincide with the Texas centennial celebrations of 1936, but the work was finished only in 1939. That opera, and another, *The Stranger of Manzano*, were premiered at North Texas.

Smith composed a number of works on Texan themes, including *Cynthia Parker* and *Remember the Alamo!*, inspired by William B. Travis' famed "Victory or Death!" letter of 1836 and composed for the inauguration of President Lyndon B. Johnson in 1965. Her sixth and final opera is one of her best-known works: *Daisy* (1973) chronicles the life of Juliette Gordon Low, who founded the Girl Scouts in the U.S.

According to the *Handbook of Texas*, her compositions "incorporate folk melodies and dance idioms within a relatively conservative, tonal harmonic palette, although she was not afraid of dissonance."

Alongside her own career as a composer, Smith also became known as an early biographer of composer Aaron Copland through the 1955 publication of her doctoral dissertation (Ph.D., NYU, 1952), *Aaron Copland: His Work and Contribution to American Music*. The Julia Smith Collection at the UNT Music Library also contains a number of scores of Copland's compositions, which she had copied by hand.

Julia Smith died in 1989 after a career as a composer, writer and advocate for women in music that covered most of the 20th century. She is buried in the Independent Order of Odd Fellows (IOOF) Cemetery in Denton. Her personal papers, compositions and other materials reside in the UNT Music Library's special collections, along with a small collection from Friedberg, her teacher and mentor.

Julia Smith at the piano, undated. *From the Julia Smith Collection* (021).

Smith conducts the Dallas Symphony, March 1940. *From the Julia Smith Collection* (021).

Smith (*seated on the left*) poses for a photograph with the creative team for her second opera, *The Stranger of Manzano*, which premiered at North Texas State Teachers College in 1945. Wilfred Bain (pictured standing behind Smith) was dean of the College of Music from 1938 to 1947.

O'Neil Ford and the North Texas Bandstand

O'Neil Ford designed many of the most iconic landmarks in Denton and is celebrated as a significant architect of the modern era. Ford designed two structures for the North Texas campus, but only one is still standing today.

O'Neil Ford (1905–1982) was born in Pink Hill, Texas, a small community near Denton. When his father died at an early age, the young Ford assumed responsibility for supporting his family and went to work as an adolescent. Ford loved to draw and showed an interest in architecture from the beginning. Ford attended North Texas for two years but was no longer able to afford tuition, so he went to work at a local diner, *Dyche's Corner*, on Avenue A, where he flipped burgers while earning his certificate in architecture through a correspondence school in Pennsylvania.

Ford had a flair for selling himself, which served him well once he began his practice as an architect. Ford's knack for business led to bigger and bigger projects, which earned him a distinguished reputation. As time passed, Ford would go on to become one of the most accomplished and noteworthy architects in Texas. In later years, he was frequently a guest speaker at colleges, where he spoke to architecture students.

Ford led the planning for such buildings as the Little Chapel in the Woods on the campus of the Texas State College for Women (now Texas Women's University) in 1939. This structure is typical of the kind of work O'Neil Ford did throughout his career, and its overall design demonstrates his philosophy on architectural structures and their practical use. Ford's other projects included the Tower of the Americas (1968) in San Antonio, First Christian Church (1987) in Denton, the Texas Instruments building (1958) in Dallas, the Civic Center Complex (1963–1968) in Denton, the Selwyn School (1967–1968) in Denton, Trinity University (1963–1971) in San Antonio and the Gazebo (1928) on the North Texas campus.

The Gazebo was built between what is now the Auditorium Building and the Language Building. Originally incorporating a fountain, today the Gazebo functions more as a place to shelter students from the elements before and after classes, a quiet spot for a break and a meeting place. Ford was always concerned with the function of his architecture as well as appearance, and even without a fountain, the Gazebo still retains some if its initial purpose as a haven for students.

Also built in 1928 was Ford's bandstand, an open-air theater constructed in the art deco or neo-classical style of the time. The bandstand was located near a swimming pool in what was then known as Eagle Park. Two years later, a projection booth, screen and speakers were added to allow showing films outdoors in addition to serving as a venue for musical performances. The bandstand only lasted for about twenty years, after which the structure was

An early postcard photograph of the gazebo with the drinking fountains still intact. *From the Mike Cochran Collection (U0718).*

The North Texas State Teachers College Band on the bandstand, 1923-1930. *From the University Photography Collection (U0458).*

An overhead view of the Gazebo near the Science Building, 1950-1959. *From the University Photography Collection (U0458).*

The Gazebo with bicycles locked to the framing, 1970-1979. *From the University Photography Collection (U0458).*

demolished to make way for the Journalism Building, which later became Scoular Hall (itself demolished in 2013 to make way for the new University Union).

A World War I memorial tower designed by Ford was planned for the North Texas campus, but it, and a planned student union, were abandoned due to a lack of funding during the Great Depression and World War II. The architectural plans show a 130-foot structure with a winding staircase including a clock with chimes, which would have replaced the campus curfew bell and served as the visual center or core of the university. North Texas did not get its bell tower until 1956, atop the Administration Building.

Ford had lifelong connections with the city of Denton, and his memories of studying the *Courthouse on the Square* during his youth stimulated a lasting interest in architecture. Ford recalled the building as fascinating him to the point of wondering, even year later, how it was ever constructed.

In 1978, the university honored Ford with the Distinguished Alumni Award. He is remembered for his influence on the architectural landscape of Texas and for helping to shape modernist architecture throughout the state.

O'Neil Ford as a student at North Texas, 1926. *From the University Photography Collection (U0458).*

In this bird's eye view, the Gazebo is visible between the Language Building and Auditorium Building while students gather on their way to classes, 1950-1960. *From the University Photography Collection (U0458).*

This portrait of Ford was taken in 1978 when he accepted the distinguished alumnus award at North Texas State University. *From the University Photography Collection (U0458).*

Music students perform on the bandstand led by their instructor, 1942. By the time of this photograph, additions to the bandstand have been incorporated into the top of the structure, most likely after 1930. Music students perform onstage led by their instructor. *From the University Photography Collection (U0458).*

Students gather around the Gazebo and water fountain, 1942. *From the University Photography Collection (U0458).*

A New Deal for North Texas

During the 1930s, enrollment at North Texas grew, but development of campus facilities was on hold due to the Great Depression. Cramped classrooms and a lack of suitable living spaces for students was the norm until a new federal funding program resulted in the construction of many of our most iconic campus buildings. If you have ever had a class in Sycamore Hall, Chilton Hall, Terrill Hall or Marquis Hall then you have benefited from the legacy of the Public Works Administration (PWA).

Starting in 1933, with the passage of the National Industrial Recovery Act, funds became available for large-scale public-works construction, such as of dams, hospitals and schools. President Weston Joseph McConnell saw an urgent need for the campus to expand during his administration, and with the authorization of the Board of Regents he applied for these federal funds to provide better academic and residential facilities for the campus.

In 1936 a new band and orchestra hall was constructed using a PWA grant and a bond issue from the Reconstruction Finance Corporation. Orchestra Hall provided classroom space as well as rooms on the top floor for thirty-six men (members of the band and orchestra) to live in. During World War II the living quarters were used by the women of the college, and after World War II the structure was used for classroom and office space.

Construction also started on a new library building 1936. The first library (now known as Curry Hall) was opened in 1912. The new library (now Sycamore Hall) opened in 1937, and a grant from the Carnegie Corporation in 1938 helped North Texas to purchase books to fill the new library. Over the years Sycamore Hall would also house a book bindery, classrooms and offices for the art department.

As North Texas grew, boarding houses were no longer adequate to accommodate the student population. Parents often requested a dormitory for women so they would not need to place their daughters in private homes. Planning began in 1934, with McConnell's wife selecting and purchasing the furnishings for this first dormitory to house 100 women. Named after recently deceased President Robert L. Marquis, it had two large dining rooms, two banquet halls, a grill and a large reception room. Once complete, some parents reversed their opinions and stated that they would rather place their daughters in a boarding house where the landlady could provide motherly attention.

UNT received PWA grants for two more dorms, one for women and one for men, in 1938. The women's dorm was named Terrill Hall, after North Texas' third president, Menter B. Terrill. The dorm had no cafeteria, so residents crossed the street to take their meals at Marquis Hall. The first dorm to be built for men was named after North Texas' first president, Joshua Crittenden Chilton. Chilton Hall was U-shaped and divided into nine units, each of which had to be accessed through its own entrance from the courtyard. For two years during World

The front of Chilton Hall, 1942. *From the University Photography Collection (U0458).*

Winding steps lead up to the Orchestra Hall. The structure housed music classrooms and office space as well as dormitory rooms for male music students on the second floor. *From the University Photography Collection (U0458).*

Terrill Hall, 1942. Originally a dormitory, the building now houses offices and classroom space for the Department of Psychology. *From the University Photography Collection (U0458).*

Seniors studying home economics lived in the Home Management House for one semester. They divided up the work of cleaning, preparing meals and other functions of running a home. A supervisor lived with them. *From the University Photography Collection (U0458).*

The wife of President Weston J. McConnell decorated the first dormitory, Marquis Hall. Chandeliers, sofas and a grand piano adorned the Hall's common room. *From the University Photography Collection (U0458).*

War II it housed the Harte Flying School. The building was renovated in the late 1980s, when the courtyard of the U-shaped structure was enclosed. It now houses offices and classrooms.

In addition, North Texas received PWA funding to construct Home Management House. This two-story brick-veneer duplex faced west on Avenue A, with West Chestnut Street to the south, and was erected in 1938 and 1939, with the PWA funding about 45% of the cost. While mainly an academic building, the house also served as the living quarters Home Economics majors. Seven women lived in each half of the house, with the supervisor having her own quarters each long semester.

While the PWA only operated until 1943, it played an important role in placing people in construction jobs at a time of high unemployment. The funds were vital in allowing North Texas to expand during the Great Depression, helping the school meet the growing demand for a college degree before and after World War II.

Picture postcard depicting the exterior of Chiton Hall. *From the Mike Cochran Collection (U0718).*

Picture postcard depicting the exterior of Terrill Hall. *From the Mike Cochran Collection (U0718).*

Picture postcard depicting the exterior of Chiton Hall. *From the Mike Cochran Collection (U0718).*

Pioneers of the Biological Sciences Program

UNT boasts outstanding biological sciences programs attracting first-class faculty and talented students from across the United States and around the world. We tend to take for granted the myriad of course offerings, superlative laboratories, grant-funded research and scholarships open to aspiring scientists. But how did we get to this point? How did a small Division of Science at the North Texas State Teachers College evolve to become a number of large departments with serious research ambitions and notable achievements to its credit?

Needless to say, all science programs—and, indeed, all university programs—are in constant flux. But change does not happen as a matter of course. More often than not, individuals appear on the scene who, for one reason or another, sense the winds of change before others and whose passion for research and teaching moves them to challenge the status quo.

Among such individuals at North Texas were limnologist Dr. Joseph Kean Gwynn Silvey (1907–1989) and microbiologist Dr. Múzquiz (born 1927). Though they arrived at North Texas within thirty years of each other, they both faced a similar problem: the absence of distinct programs in their respective fields and the paucity of funding and equipment for research. With enthusiasm and single-minded determination, they worked tirelessly to create an academic environment that would allow them and their students to conduct high-quality research.

Walk by the fountain of the Environmental Education, Science and Technology Building, and you will encounter a life-size bronze statue of a man seated on the side of the pond. "Doc" Silvey, a nationally and internationally recognized limnologist and Distinguished Professor Emeritus, served as the chair of the Department of Biological Sciences from 1952 to 1973. Undoubtedly, the very presence of this statue speaks to the importance of the man whose likeness it renders. Indeed, Silvey played a crucial role in making the Department of Biological Sciences what it is today.

Silvey joined the faculty of North Texas State Teachers College in 1935, when biology was part of the Division of Science (which also included physics and chemistry) and when the highest degree offered to biology students was that of Bachelor of Science. A passionate researcher and dedicated educator, the professor spearheaded UNT's water research program, founding the Center for Environmental Studies (later the Institute of Applied Science) in 1970. From 1971 to 1975 he also served as associate dean of basic sciences of what was then the Texas College of Osteopathic Medicine. Silvey played a decisive role in TCOM becoming the UNT Health Science Center, for which he received the Founder's Award from TCOM in 1989.

Over his long tenure at North Texas, Silvey taught and mentored legions of students. Indefatigable in securing important research grants, he created valuable opportunities for researching the water quality of lakes and water

J.K.G. Silvey, date unknown. *From the University Photography Collection (U0458).*

Staff of the Department of Biology, including Silvey, circa 1942. *From the University Photography Collection (U0458).*

A biology student at UNT. *From the University Photography Collection (U0458).*

supply systems in Texas and Oklahoma. As chair of the University's pre-medical and pre-dental advisory committee, he thoughtfully guided students in their career choices and wrote an untold number of recommendations, which helped many gain entrance to medical and dental schools.

Silvey's students admired him for his professional achievements and deeply appreciated his kindness and support. In recognition of the profound effect he had on their lives, a group of students and colleagues established J. K. G. Silvey Society in 1965. In 2015, 26 years after Dr. Silvey's passing, the Silvey Honor Society continues to provide assistance to many future scientists and doctors.

Vela, now Professor Emeritus of biology, arrived at North Texas in 1965, when the university had no adequate science laboratories, little funding and no serious investment in building science programs of regional or national significance. It was only thanks to Vela's passion for science, love of teaching and determination that he succeeded in laying the foundation of the university's microbiology program. A noted scientist, nationally and internationally recognized for his study of nitrogen-fixing bacteria and research in bacterial physiology, Dr. Vela mentored his students with full dedication and over a period of 35 years supervised 45 master's and 19 doctoral theses. A sought-after visiting professor at American and foreign universities, a member of prestigious professional organizations and a frequent participant at national and international conferences, he introduced his students to regional and national science organizations and encouraged them to attend professional conferences. Concerned by the small representation of minorities in the student body at the university, Vela also led initiatives to improve minority students' academic performance at the elementary and high school levels.

Vela's students have often expressed their wholehearted gratitude for his guidance and unwavering support. In 2014, more than 20 microbiology alumni from across the U.S. and abroad organized a reunion honoring their beloved Professor. One of his former students, who continued research on bacteria isolated earlier by Dr. Vela, proposed it be named after Vega: *Paenibacillus velaei*.

Besides his work in microbiology, Vela has been a dedicated community leader and a published writer on the history of Mexico. In recognition of his life achievements, Latino Monthly listed him in their millennium edition as one of the top 100 Texas Latinos of the 20th century.

It is apparent that these two faculty members shared some salient qualities: passion for research, enthusiasm for teaching and determination coupled with inexhaustible energy. Early on, they came to understand the importance of research in university education. True visionaries, they succeeded in creating two important biological sciences programs at North Texas: limnology and microbiology. Today, their colleagues and students continue to build on the foundations they laid.

Gerard Roland Vela Múzquiz at work. *From the University Photography Collection (U0458).*

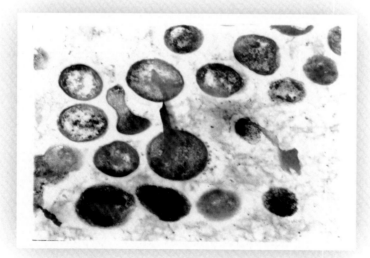

Vela's collection includes images taken from slides of his work researching nitrogen-fixing bacteria and bacterial physiology. *From the Gerald Roland Vela Múzquiz Papers (AR0447).*

North Texas and World War II

The Campus during Wartime

Following the attack on Pearl Harbor in 1941, the United States declared war on Japan, entering World War II. North Texas students and faculty gathered in the Main Auditorium to hear President Roosevelt's address to the nation. North Texas President W.J. McConnell's annual address in the 1941–1942 *Yucca* yearbook was somber but hopeful. The message was clear: North Texas was prepared to pledge all it could to ensure a "full and complete victory but also to the achievement of a just and enduring peace."

Like much of the world during this momentous time, the college began to anticipate the shifts in daily life due to the mounting pressures of war. It was a grave time for those attending classes as declaration of war meant focusing fully on enlistment as well as on campaigns and programs for war relief. In 1941, coursework was offered through the Civilian Pilot Training Program, officer training programs, the Army Specialized Training Program and other federal programs to contribute as much manpower and resources to the war effort as possible.

The federal government established the Civilian Pilot Training Program in 1939. In October 1940, twenty North Texas students from differing class levels were enrolled in a ground and flight training course covering aerial navigation, meteorology, civil-air regulations, flight training and the standard service of aircraft. Students received six credit hours towards their degree for course completion.

After the success of the first course, enrollment for the spring increased to forty students, three of whom were women. At the end of the spring session in June 1941, twenty-eight students, including two women, received their pilot's license. An estimated three hundred students received training before the program was discontinued in 1942 and replaced by another program, in which North Texas hosted fifteen naval aeronautics trainees and, at any given time, up to sixty-five naval cadets. These trainees received their basic training on campus and were taught ground courses by the faculty. Though the Navy unit ceased operations in 1943, an Army unit commenced flight training and became the last class to complete coursework in the Civil Aeronautics Administration program.

In addition, North Texas instituted eight officer training programs for students. Faculty directed these programs and oversaw individual development of the students. Those accepted to the reserve programs progressed through the program until completion or until they were called to active duty. Three hundred students were enrolled in the various reserves curriculum by December of 1942.

Members of the Women's Defense Corps participate
in fire-drill training, circa 1940s. *From the University
Photography Collection (U0458).*

Students in the Civilian Pilot Training Program, circa 1940s. *From the University
Photography Collection (U0458).*

Students line up at the post office to buy war bonds, circa 1940s. *From the
University Photography Collection (U0458).*

The Army Specialized Training Program was offered at UNT beginning in July 1943 with 250 trainees. Living in portable barracks initially, the trainees were eventually moved to Chilton Hall. Sixteen faculty members provided instruction in pre-engineering, pre-medical, pre-dental, humanities and science programs. Army trainees also participated in intramural activities including a cadet glee club, sports and literary competitions. In November 1943, a second consignment of trainees began coursework in the program, replacing those who did not keep pace with the demands of the rigorous program. When the unit was dissolved in March 1944, North Texas was ranked in the upper third by enrollment of all colleges in the country with similar programs.

In 1943, as the war campaigns in both the European and Pacific theaters were vigorously fought, the *Yucca* yearbook reflected the all-encompassing effect of the war on the home front. The yearbook's cover design—rows of helmeted soldiers marching towards an invisible enemy beyond the cover—is symbolic for all the soldiers leaving North Texas and their educational pursuits to fight. War relief campaigns on campus, documented in the pages of the yearbook and bulletins, included blood drives, knitting drives, Red Cross first aid classes, food drives and victory concerts featuring student and faculty performers.

While World War II tested the North Texas students and faculty with challenges to meet both the educational and war relief demands, President McConnell's wartime message rings true to this day: "It is time for sober thinking and not for emotional outbursts. The world is going through a struggle, an agony, today that we hope will be the last of its kind in history."

Soldiers march past Theatre Row (Elm Street) on the Denton Courthouse Square, 1942. *From the University Photography Collection (U0458).*

Women enrolled in an industrial arts class, circa 1940s. *From the University Photography Collection (U0458).*

A couple talking in the bleachers of the first football field, now the location of the Library Mall, circa 1940s. *From the University Photography Collection (U0458).*

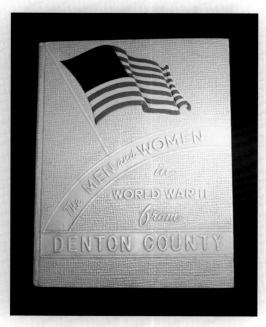

The Denton chapter of the American Legion published this book circa 1945.

Raza at UNT

Latino/a students are an important part of university life but were not visible as a distinctive group until April of 1970, when they formed the first Latino/a group on campus. According to the 1971 *Yucca* yearbook, "Los Chicanos" was formed to "meet the social, cultural and educational needs of Mexican-American students." While the university created the Center for Ethnic Affairs in 1974 to provide better support for minority members of the community, that year only 300 students were Hispanic, and they were referred to as the "forgotten minority" on campus in that year's *Yucca*. Los Chicanos, then known as MASA, made it a priority to "return on a yearly basis to many of Texas' poor Mexican-American neighborhoods . . . to provide and establish with younger students a positive identification factor with life in a white university." This remained the only Latino/a group on campus for close to twenty years, going through many name changes, including La Causa, the Mexican American Student Association (MASA), the Mexican American Student Organization (MASO), Hispanic Students for Higher Education (HSHE) and the Association of Latino American Students (ALAS).

Throughout the years, Latino/a students made regular appearances in the *Yucca*. One of the earliest Latina students at the university, hailing from Puerto Rico, was Maria Isabel Rodriguez Quetglas. She was popularly known as Betty Rodriguez and graduated with a B.A. in Spanish in 1943. She was a member of the Gammadions and was the Junior and Senior Miss Ardens. As president of the Pan-American Forum she worked to promote education about Latin America and the Spanish language and served as hostess at the Spanish table in Marquis Hall Dining Room to help fellow students practice their Spanish. In 1942 she was appointed second lieutenant of Company B in the newly formed North Texas State Defense Training Battalion of the Women's Defense Corps. This defense corps was the only known women's training unit in the country and made up entirely of students with the goal of training women to be leaders in defense organizations around the state.

Victor Rodríguez ('55) was the first Hispanic scholarship athlete and the first Hispanic letterman in North Texas history. In his senior year, Rodríguez was the secretary of the Geezles fraternity, a member of both the Varsity Track and Sprint Medley Relay Teams, and recipient of a track scholarship. Rodríguez was also featured in the "Who's Who" section of the 1955 *Yucca*.

Rodríguez earned a B.A. in art education in 1955 and returned to earn an M.A. in education in 1962. After completing his Ph.D. at the University of Texas, Dr. Rodríguez became the first Mexican American school superintendent in San Antonio, where he was honored with numerous awards during his tenure. His autobiography *The Bell Ringer* was published in 2005, and he was inducted into the North Texas Athletic Hall of Fame in 2006.

Los Chicanos was the first Hispanic group formed on campus, in 1970. *Yucca*, 1970.

Juan Estrada, member of the North Texas golf team and Mexican National Amateur Open Tournament champion. *Yucca*, 1958.

Victor Rodriguez runs during a track and field event in 1955. *From the Victor Rodriguez Papers (U0205).*

Dr. Rodríguez graciously donated his personal papers to the Special Collections department of the UNT Libraries. The collection includes his Varsity letter jacket and several medals, photographs and clippings illustrating his numerous achievements.

Latino faculty have also had a major impact on UNT history. In 1987, Dr. Gloria Contreras was hired as the first Chicana professor at North Texas. Within a month of her arrival she was chosen to serve as faculty sponsor of MASO. In 1989 she was appointed the first director of the Office of Minority Affairs (now the Multicultural Center) by President Alfred F. Hurley, where she was charged with creating and implementing a five-year plan for the recruitment, retention and graduation of minority students and faculty. As a result of her successful initiatives, over twenty cultural student organizations are active on campus today.

2012 was a banner year for Latino/a students. The Latino/a student population increased by 11.4 percent from the previous year to 6,093, and UNT held its first Raza graduation. This involved a bilingual ceremony to bring cultural awareness and celebrate Latino culture and heritage. For Hispanic Heritage Month, the UNT Libraries held a symposium and the Special Collections department sponsored an exhibit titled "Raíces: Raza History at UNT."

Maria Isabel Rodriguez Quetglas, more popularly known as Betty Rodriguez, was a Spanish major from Puerto Rico. She received her B.A. in 1943 and can be seen here looking through a card catalog. She was president of the Pan-American Forum and acted as a translator for visiting dignitaries. *From the University Photography Collection (U0458).*

Dr. Gloria Contreras in her office, year unknown. *From the University Photography Collection (U0458).*

Sweatshirt worn by members of the Mexican American Student Organization (MASO). A "no grapes" button on the sweatshirt refers to the 1965–1970 United Farm Workers strike to improve working conditions in Californian vineyards. *From the University Artifacts Collection (U0493).*

Fry Street

A Home Away from Home

From the early 1980s to 2007, the Brotherhood of the Delta Lodge, an independent fraternity who called themselves "the party professionals," organized the Fry Street Fair. This event was an annual gathering for students and the community to share laughs, enjoy refreshments and dance to the melodies of local and regional bands. The fair also showcased the sociocultural significance of the Fry Street area to the University of North Texas. This area has always been a home away from home for students.

Prior to the Fry Street Fair, this area, comprised of Fry, Hickory and Mulberry Streets, was a hub for students. In the late 1940s and 1950s, students could walk across campus to purchase clothing and shoes, school supplies and other personal necessities from Fry Street businesses. If shopping was not on the agenda, North Texas students could gather with their dates to share sodas or a meal at Hamilton Drug Store.

In the 1960s and 1970s, Fry Street transformed into a center for a new and growing subculture. Hippies, free spirits and "long hairs" enjoyed visiting specialized shops such as Clear Light Books and the Head Shop and grabbing some grub at Jim's Diner, the Flying Tomato or Star's Restaurant. It was at this time that Fry Street gained a new counterculture identity.

With 1970s counterculture firmly established in the Fry Street area, the 1980s brought with it the Delta Lodge, their "Sammie House" on the corner of West Oak Street and Fry Street, and the Fry Street Fair. Originally part of the Sigma Mu Alpha national fraternity, the Delta Lodge became their own non-profit organization in the mid-1980s after receiving official recognition from the state of Texas. As advocates of the local music and arts scene, the brothers of this organization saw something unique in this area where students congregated before and after classes, and they wanted to celebrate the independent and eclectic spirit of Fry Street.

The Fry Street fair was the idea of Delta Lodge brothers (and alumni) David Biles, David Vied and Micheal Sitrin. The idea was brought up during a Monday night meeting, with one of the brothers reflecting on a recent arts and craft fair he attended. He thought that the fraternity could be successful in throwing a similar event, and as they were always looking for original ways to throw a party, all of the brothers agreed on the idea. After many discussions about the fair throughout the semester, Biles and Sitrin decided it was time to think about logistics; city permit applications were in order and Fry Street business owners needed to approve the event.

Arts & Entertainment

The North Texas Daily

Page 5 — Thursday, April 23, 1987

Sammies gear up for eighth Fry Street Fair

President says outlook good despite absence of alcohol vendors

Tommy Rocker rolls into festival

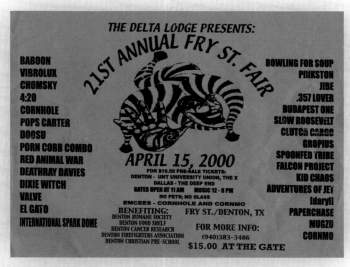

The 8th annual fair was featured in this *North Texas Daily* article from 1987.

A flyer advertising the 21st annual Fry Street Fair hosted by the Delta Lodge in April 2000.

Fry Street Develops as Center of Emerging Subculture

'Freaks' Run Businesses in Free Life Style

The *North Texas Daily* reported on Fry Street's emerging subculture in 1970.

Generations shape neighborhood

The *North Texas Daily* printed this retrospective on Fry Street's history in 2007.

The first fair was straightforward. Held at Sammie House, it featured six bands and was attended by 1,500 students and community members. Held each year until 2007, this event served as a vehicle for the fraternity to give back to the community. From booking local and regional bands to giving the local Fry Street businesses a fiscal boost, the Delta Lodge donated the money they received from fair attendees to the United Way of Denton, the Willis Library and other local charities.

Fry Street remains a home for UNT students. The area reflects social changes, both local and national. Today, it's a place for gathering over a strong cup of joe at 3 a.m. to cram before an 8 a.m. final, for grabbing a quick lunch, for buying books or art supplies, for viewing local art and murals and for people-watching. It's also a place of collective memory where ghosts of long-gone businesses and people linger in the air.

Students enjoy sodas at the Hamilton Drug Store, circa 1940s–1950s. *From the University Photography Collection (U0458).*

Students wait in line to order food at the Flying Tomato, circa 1980s. *From the University Photography Collection (U0458).*

Fry Street with view of head shop sign, circa 1972. *From the University Photography Collection (U0458).*

The interior of a head shop located on Fry Street, circa 1972. *From the University Photography Collection (U0458).*

Evolution of the Student Union

A central place to rest, meet friends and have fun was the wish of early North Texas students who did not have a student union on campus for many years. This wish was delayed due to financial difficulties brought on by the Great Depression and World War II. Following the war, North Texas entered a building boom to better serve the increased enrollment due to returning soldiers; a student union was one of the structures added to the campus. It served as a gathering place for students and also a more somber function as a memorial to the students who gave their lives in the world wars. It was named the Student Memorial Union Building.

The structure was originally used as an army service center at Camp Bowie near Brownwood, Texas, before being moved to campus and rebuilt as a student union building. The structure faced West Chestnut Street and was two stories high, with a large veranda in the center of the south (rear) side. The building boasted a snack bar, cafeteria, dance-lounge area, club rooms, an auditorium, game rooms, a post office and offices for the director and staff.

The union was dedicated on March 31, 1949, the fiftieth anniversary of the signing of the legislation that made UNT a state institution in 1899. Roger M. Ramey of the US Air Force spoke to a gathering of administrators, faculty and students at the ceremony. A bronze plaque was erected in the main foyer listing the names of the former students who died in military service.

The main gathering space, called the "Howdy Room," was in the center of the union. It was decorated with a western theme. A cement slab ("the Slab") adjacent to the union served as a place to hold dances (such as the Wednesday night dances and the Howdy Dance) and an informal gathering spot for students.

By 1961, the union was no longer large enough to accommodate the growing student population. Plans were made to build a new student union in two stages. First, in 1963, the Slab was broken up and removed to make way for the construction of the first wing of the new union. When that wing opened in 1964, the first union was torn down to make way for the construction of the second wing of the new union.

The new building had three stories with a brick veneer. The first part to open contained a post office, which boasted 7,621 mailboxes. The new union also contained a trophy room, a lounge, a cafeteria and the University Bookstore. By 1969, six pool tables were installed in the main lounge on the third floor, and around this time the trophy room was turned into a TV lounge.

The second union was not yet ten years old when the university started to plan an expansion of the building. The new structure would encircle part of the 1960s structure and more than double the space. The plan to expand the union building was approved by the Board of Regents in 1973, and the work on the expansion started in May of that year. However, the opening of the third union, planned for fall 1975, was delayed due to labor strikes but

The front of the second union building as it appeared as construction on the structure was nearing completion, circa 1965. *From the University Photography Collection (U0458).*

The east side of the third union building, 1991. The kiosks stood near the entrances to the building. They were covered with notices of upcoming events, new course offerings, advertisements for new roommates and sale notices. *From the University Photography Collection (U0458).*

Postal workers fill the student mail boxes in the second union, circa 1960s. *From the University Photography Collection (U0458).*

Students gather in the central courtyard in the third union, circa 1976. One of the unique features of this area was a "river" fountain, which was set below the level of the floor. The rushing water provided a peaceful background sounds to the area. *From the University Photography Collection (U0458).*

The first union building was dedicated on March 31, 1949. Roger M. Ramey, an officer in the Air Force and North Texas alumnus, was the guest speaker at the event. He recalled his days as a student twenty-five years earlier and how the students at that time longed for a union. He stated that he did not think then that the students would need to wait through another world war before they would see the dream fulfilled. *From the University Photography Collection (U0458).*

was eventually dedicated on March 7, 1976, and called the North Texas State University Union. Built on four levels, the new structure included new dining facilities, meeting rooms, a 300-seat theater and a suite of offices for student services. An arts and crafts room was provided on the lower level.

One of the striking visual elements in the third union was the fiber art that hung on the wall in the main indoor courtyard. The creation of internationally renowned artist Françoise Grossen, this rope sculpture was built using a single overhand knot as the only structural element to create the fiber work measuring 30 × 16 feet. It was named Tensile Ten because there were five points at the top and five at the bottom where the artwork was attached to the wall of the union.

The rooms in the third union received names that reflected the history of the university:

The *Campus Chat* was named after the first campus newspaper, first published in 1916. This area served as a food service area.

The **Corner** was named after the shopping area on West Hickory Street and Avenue A (known to today's students as the Fry Street area). The Corner provided snacks to hungry students, including ice cream, soft drinks, fruit, sandwiches and candy.

One O'Clock Lounge was named after the premiere lab band in the College of Music. It was an open lounge with terraced seating located next to the southeast door.

The **Syndicate** was named after the group of Denton businessmen who organized the founding of the school and acquired the land in 1890 and 1891.

The **Avesta** was named for a student literary journal first published in 1917. Originally the Avesta was the name of a first-floor lounge for studying and listening to music. The lounge was altered into seating for a food court, and the name was redeployed for a dining facility on the second floor of the union.

The **Lyceum**, the theater in the union, was named for the first fine-arts programs, known as "lyceum numbers," presented by UNT in the early 20th century.

The **Golden Eagle Suite** honored alumni who graduated more than 50 years ago.

The **Silver Eagle Room** honored alumni who graduated more than 25 years ago.

The **Denton Suite**, a cluster of three rooms, was named for three members of the Syndicate: W. A. Ponder, John A. Hann and T. W. Abney.

The third union was demolished in 2013 to make way for construction of the fourth union, which opened in 2015.

A view of the University Bookstore in the second union, where students could find office supplies, desk lamps, art supplies, magazines, jewelry, as well as text books. *From the University Photography Collection (U0458).*

NTSU coffee cup. *From the University Artifacts Collection (U0493).*

Each spring the university community celebrated having a student union with Union Day. This image is dated 1996. *From the University Photography Collection (U0458).*

Commemorative NTSU University Union medallion, 1976. *From the University Artifacts Collection (U0493).*

NTSU University Union matchbook with the 1976 union logo. *From the University Artifacts Collection (U0493).*

Desegregation in the Classroom and on the Football Field

The mid-1950s marked a crucial point in the history of education and civil rights in America. During this time North Texas State College, like most educational institutions, was spurred to action by the 1954 *Brown v. Board of Education* Supreme Court verdict, which found segregated schools to be unconstitutional. Although the first African American graduate student, A. Tennyson Miller, was admitted to NTSC in 1954, it was not until 1956 that Irma E. L. Sephas, the first African American undergraduate student, was admitted to the college.

While it has been known for many years that Sephas was a trailblazer at UNT, it was only recently that we have been able to see images of this historic time on campus. Footage of her first week on campus was recently discovered by UNT Libraries staff within the NBC 5 / KXAS (WBAP) Television News Collection, which was donated to the UNT Libraries in 2013. Prior to this discovery there was no known image of Sephas as a student on campus.

University administration feared that Sephas would face riots or violence on campus similar to events unfolding at University of Alabama. However, as seen on this footage, her first days at UNT passed peacefully, with Sephus saying on film, "I am happy to be a student on the campus of good old North Texas that exemplifies the true Texas spirit, because certainly every hour that I have spent here has been a pleasant one."

This unique footage belies the turmoil that at times surrounded desegregation at UNT. It is known from later interviews that President James Carl Matthews dispatched crews to campus in the early morning hours to erase racial epithets that had been chalked on sidewalks and to extinguish a burning cross on the lawn of the Administrative Building.

In the following semester of 1956, Abner Haynes and Leon King became symbols of North Texas integration when they became the first two African American football players to play for the NTSC football team.

Haynes grew up the son a well-known Denton minister and attended Lincoln High School in Dallas, where he befriended teammate Leon King. Although NTSC had integrated, the college had no black athletes. President Matthews told Coach Odus Mitchell that any African American students who showed interest in the football team should be given a fair chance. Haynes and King were given a tryout and awarded a half scholarship to play on the freshman football team, but they were not allowed to live on campus or eat in the dining halls for the first two years they were at college.

The pivotal event that cemented their relationship with their teammates was an away game during the 1956 season against Navarro Junior College in Corsicana, Texas. Before the game the team went out to eat at a restaurant,

Abner Haynes made a 51-yard run back on the
kickoff against Cincinnati, as shown in this photo
from the 1959 *Yucca* yearbook.

Haynes' official picture from the
1959 *Yucca* yearbook.

Still image of Irma Sephas taken from original 16mm film of her first week on
campus. *From the NBC 5 / KXAS (WBAP) Television News Collection (AR0776).*

and King and Haynes were told they had to eat in the kitchen. Their teammates stood behind them and said they would not eat at the restaurant unless they could all eat together. They ended up eating baloney sandwiches, and the restaurant lost revenue from meals prepared in advance for the team.

When they arrived at the game the crowd was hostile, yelling racial epithets and death threats, not just against the black players, but also against their white teammates for allowing them to play. This hostility spurred the team into playing harder, and North Texas tackle Joe Mack Pryor went out of his way to knock down any other player who treated the two black players badly. They defeated the favored Navarro Junior College 39 to 21, with Haynes running four touchdowns and King catching a pass for a score. Coach Ken Bahnsen had told the bus driver to park close to the field, and at the end of the game he ordered the players to run for the bus as soon as the game ended. The white team players surrounded King and Haynes and ran to the waiting bus. Haynes said in a later oral history interview that the angry crowd did them a favor because it brought the team together, whereas otherwise the team players might have fought among themselves. He added, "We were scared to death, but that team became a family that day in Corsicana." In his own oral history King said, "We became blood brothers. . . . What affected one of us, affected all of us."

Linemen 'Do Hardest Work,'
According to Star Halfback

by JIMMY JONES

After the Navarro game in Corsicana, which the Eagles won 28-21, Coach Ken Bahnsen began calling in the game report to the Dallas Morning News. He asked a group of players nearby:

"Who made the touchdowns?"

"I think Abner [Haynes] made four," one of the boys said.

"How many touchdowns did you score, Abner?" Bahnsen asked.

The Lincoln high, Dallas, speedster scratched his head and thought for a moment.

"You'd better ask the linemen about that," he said. "They're the ones who did all the work—all I did was run when I saw daylight."

Abner reflects the philosophy of the coach who says, "Anyone can run with the ball as long as all of the tacklers are knocked down."

Tennis Anyone?

"There will be a short, important meeting in the men's gym Wednesday at 6:00 p.m. for all boys interested in either varsity or freshman tennis," Coach Bahnsen, tennis sponsor, said Thursday.

Returning varsity lettermen are Charles Wieux, Richard Matlock, and Louis Compton.

Eagle tennis teams will play in the MVC next spring. Cincinnati is expected to give the Flock rough competition. Tony Trabert, perhaps

the top tennis man in the nation, graduated from Cincinnati a few years ago.

Rough Links Conference

With their entrance into the MVC the Eagle golfers will have a good conference to play in. Last year's NCAA champion, the University of Houston, will be ready to give North Texas a rough time. Led by Rex Baxter Jr., the Cougars edged Coach Herb Ferrill's linksters for the national crown last summer.

World Series TV

Walk through the UB anytime this week and you will see a cheering crowd of baseball fans. They're watching the World series on TV. Brooklyn and Yankee fans place their bets before the game begins and then really enter into the spirit of the contest. You'd think the crowd was actually in Yankee stadium as they boo the umpires and plead with Mickey Mantle to "get a hit." We're expecting someone to get carried away and throw a Coke bottle at the umpire.

Touch Football

For real action you can't beat intramural football. Several teams get into play this week, and many fraternity men and independents have sore muscles and skinned elbows.

This article from the *Campus Chat* on October 5, 1956, is the only contemporary mention in NTSC's newspaper of the Corsicana game. Haynes reveals a good sense of humor, giving the linemen all the credit and downplaying his own role in leading his team to victory.

Haynes running down the field with the ball in this photo from the *North Texas Daily*, February 13, 2004.

Images from a 1958 NTSC football program featuring players including Haynes and King.

Images from a 1958 NTSC football program featuring players including Haynes and King.

Where the Mean Green Are Seen

From Fouts Field to Apogee Stadium

On September 10, 2011, the Mean Green took the field against the University of Houston Cougars in UNT's first home game at the newly constructed Apogee Stadium. Over 28,000 fans were in attendance that day; the game marked the third highest attendance for an on-campus home game.

The previous home of the Mean Green was Fouts Field. Originally named Eagle Stadium when it opened in 1952, it was renamed two years later in honor of former North Texas Normal School football coach and athletic director Theron J. Fouts. The field originally featured sideline seating on both sides of the field with a total capacity of 20,000. Though not the first football facility on campus, Fouts would be the location of North Texas home games for fifty-eight years.

The Eagles' first game at Fouts Field was a 55–0 victory over the University of North Dakota Fighting Sioux (now the UND Fighting Hawks). During their time at Fouts Field, the Mean Green won twenty five conference championships—eight in the Lonestar Conference, five in the Gulf Coast Conference, six in the Missouri Valley Conference, two in the Southland Conference and four in the Sun Belt Conference—and had five bowl game appearances, including the 2002 win over the University of Cincinnati Bearcats in the New Orleans Bowl. The largest crowd ever seen at Fouts Field was during the 1990 centennial homecoming show produced by Starlight Entertainment of Dallas.

In later decades the field's modest accommodations made it difficult for the Eagles to attract teams from larger schools to play in Denton. In order to accommodate larger crowds, in 1971 UNT began playing select home games at Texas Stadium in Irving. In 1987, the Board of Regents entered into a ten-year contract with the Denton Independent School District to improve Fouts Field, including the addition of artificial turf, so that the field could be used for both collegiate and high-school athletic activities. Further improvements came in 1991, when Bill Miller, president of the Student Association, proposed a student-funded project to add endzone seating to Fouts to increase its capacity to 30,000.

Still, UNT needed a new stadium. In 2002, UNT students held a referendum on whether the North Texas System Board of Regents should increase the student athletics fee by $4.50 per credit hour, with $1 of the increase going toward facility improvements that would include a new stadium. The referendum was defeated 1,265 to 1,023, but school administrators lobbied for an increase in order to bring the school into compliance with Title IX.

Aerial view of Fouts Field, undated. *From the University Photography Collection (U0458).*

UNT's Charles Edward "Mean Joe" Greene, 1967. *From the University Photography Collection (U0458).*

Theron J. Fouts views the blueprints for the future Fouts Field, circa 1950s. *From the University Photography Collection (U0458).*

Groundbreaking for the Fouts Field renovation, 1994. *Left to right*: Denton Mayor Bob Castleberry, Regent R. L. Crawford, Student Association President Jasen Miller, Regent Joe Kirven, Athletic Trustee President Ed Whittemore and former Student Association President Bill Miller. *From the University Photography Collection (U0458).*

The student government voted for an increase of $3 per credit hour, which the Board of Regents accepted. This resulted in UNT students mounting a recall election campaign, which removed fourteen student senators.

The following fall, UNT purchased land from Liberty Christian School adjacent to UNT's golf course in order to construct the Mean Green Village, a collection of new athletic facilities including a new stadium. Another student referendum on a dedicated athletics fee to support the new stadium and other athletics-program improvements was held in October 2008. The proposed fee of $7 per credit hour was approved by a vote of 2,829 to 2,038, one of the largest turnouts for a student election in UNT history.

Construction began in November 2009. The new $78 million stadium was designed by HKS Sports and Entertainment Group. Amenities included seating for more than 30,000 fans, sixteen concession stands and a Mean Green team store. The Mean Green continued to play at Fouts Field until the end of 2010 season. Naming rights to the new stadium (originally called simply "Mean Green Stadium") were purchased in 2011 by Austin, TX-based Apogee, provider of ResNet LAN services for higher education.

Apogee Stadium's association with "green" goes beyond football, though: it is the first collegiate stadium to receive LEED Platinum certification from the U.S. Green Building Council. The stadium's design features the use of non-toxic paints, recycled and locally manufactured construction materials, landscaping with plants and trees native to the North Texas region and permeable pavers to reduce stormwater runoff. Furthermore, around 10% of its energy consumption is generated by three wind turbines. UNT President V. Lane Rawlins called the new stadium "a great accomplishment for UNT," which "strongly underscores our commitment to sustainability."

Freshman quarterback Austin McNulty scored the first touchdown in in the new stadium. Unfortunately, the Mean Green lost to the Cougars that day, 48–23. Attendance for the new stadium's inaugural year averaged 18,864, over 60% of the stadium's capacity. The Mean Green finished the 2011 season 5–7, 4–4 in conference play.

Fouts Field is planned for demolition to make way for two residence halls, a parking garage and a university opera house.

The Mean Green enter Apogee Stadium during the 2013 homecoming game against the University of Texas at El Paso. *From the Junebug Clark University Photo Collection (AR0814).*

The Eagles in the 1992 homecoming game against the Demons of Northwestern State University in Louisiana. *From the University Photography Collection (U0458).*

Sunbelt Championship medallion. *From the University Artifacts Collection (U0493).*

Souvenir fan from the 2011 season at the new football stadium. Prior to adopting the Apogee name, the stadium was known simply as "Mean Green Stadium." *From the Brenda K. Ritz Collection (U0719).*

Commemorative coin celebrating the Inaugural Game at Apogee Stadium, September 10, 2011. *From the University Artifacts Collection (U0493).*

Football program from the 2010 "Fouts Field Finale" season. *From the Brenda K. Ritz Collection (U0719).*

A Mammoth Find for Students

1953 was a big year for paleontological finds near Denton. The Denton County Archaeology Society formed after the discovery of a mastodon tooth cap near Lake Dallas. Society members also joined together to locate and save archeological artifacts from inundation when the Garza-Little Elm Dam opened in October 1953.

In early 1953, Ernest M. Calvert Jr. discovered mammoth bones protruding from a seven-foot arroyo on his father's farm, located five miles south of Denton. Calvert contacted North Texas State College (NTSC) about the find and gave permission for NTSC students and faculty to spend Saturdays excavating the partial mammoth skeleton. NTSC faculty members Carl B. Compton (art) and Elgin Williams (sociology) and a total of fifty students excavated the mammoth using trowels and whisk brooms from February to April 1953. Members of the public were welcome to visit the dig site from 2 to 5 p.m. each Saturday. In-between digs a sign was installed to warn off anyone who might tamper with the dig site. It read "Do Not Molest / This Elephant Is Being Excavated For Scientific Purposes. / Please Do Not Touch or Remove."

The Saturday digs are documented in a series of images titled "Mammoth Excavation" in the 1953 Yucca yearbook, with deadpan captions underneath images of students carefully exhuming the mammoth. "He's awfully big—and awfully dead," reads one. "No bones about it. This is work," reads another.

The mammoth, a Parelephas columbi, was estimated to be ten feet tall, twenty feet long and two to three tons in weight when it died 10,000 years earlier. Examination of the mammoth's teeth revealed it probably died at the young age of 70 (out of a potential 200-year lifespan). University of Texas archaeologist Alex Perry Kreiger rated the specimen the best discovered in Texas to date. R. K. Harris of the Dallas Archaeology Society believed it to be the most complete skeleton in North Texas because it was exposed by natural erosion and not destructive construction equipment.

As reported in the *Campus Chat* on April 17, 1953, the Manual Arts Building (razed in 1974 and replaced by the current Art Building on West Mulberry Street) was converted into a "cave room" to display the recovered mammoth bones, along with other exhibits "trac[ing] a chronological succession of county culture through the ages." Space was probably available for the "cave room" due to departments moving out of the Manual Arts Building into their own dedicated buildings.

In March 1953, an Archaeology Festival, timed to coincide with Fine Arts Week, was held by the students involved with excavating the mammoth, and a picnic was held on March 27 at the dig site at the Calvert Farm.

The Calvert Farm mammoth was not the first or last to be discovered in the Dallas–Fort Worth area. Another mammoth was previously uncovered in 1951, 1.5 miles southeast of the 1953 site, and another in 2014, south of Dallas.

Over the years, the Special Collections department has been asked several times where the mammoth is now. The truth is that we don't know. Nothing like a little mystery alongside your pre-history!

The mammoth bones are buried deep. Dig on.

Campusites unearthed a 10,000 year-old prehistoric mammoth elephant this spring and came up with the best preserved specimen in North Texas.

The mammoth, whose scientific name is parelephas columbi, lived in the pleistocene age and died at the age of 70, during its prime. It measured 20 feet long and ten feet high.

Partially exposed bones were discovered in December on the Ernest M. Calvert farm near Denton. Student and faculty excavating parties, equipped with whisk brooms and trowels, found a part of the skull, pelvis, two leg bones, a vertebrae and a ten-foot tusk.

Out of town sight-seers and a Dallas Archaeology society member viewed the elephant.

Just in case someone is desperate for a dead elephant.

Mammoth Excavation

No bones about it. This is work.

The book says it died of prehistoric alcoholism.

The tusk of the mammoth is nine feet long.

He's awfully big—and awfully dead.

Pages from 1953 *Yucca* yearbook documenting the mammoth dig.

Unclaimed Jewels

Celebrating Old Maid's Day

A group of women in Denton started Old Maid's Day in 1950 to get "recognition, not menfolks." It all began when Miss Dorothy Babb, a Latin and English teacher at North Texas State College, was tired of buying gifts for weddings, Mother's Day and baby showers. She complained to Mrs. Dude Neville McCloud, the NTSC news service director, that it was unfair that she only got gifts at Christmas and had spent over $1,500 buying gifts for others. On a lark Mrs. McCloud wrote a feature for the Associated Press, which was published in newspapers all over the United States and eventually overseas asking for recognition and gifts for women who either couldn't or refused to get married.

Denton Mayor Mark Hannah designated Tuesday, August 15, 1950, a day to honor unmarried women. People suggested more flattering names for these women such as glamor girls, unclaimed blessings, unclaimed jewels, career girls, unmarried ladies or bachelor girls, but Miss Babb said that she just preferred being called an old maid. "Anybody who didn't like the name [old maid] could just go and get married."

The first year's celebration included a tea at the Denton Country Club and free admission to a show featuring 'Fessor Floyd Graham and his orchestra and films including the Three Stooges in The Brideless Groom at the Campus Theater, which also provided free soft drinks, popcorn and candy. In addition, gifts were provided for distribution to any unmarried woman who would admit to being an old maid.

In 1951 the event for the "unclaimed jewels" grew to 350 attendees for tea, 'Fessor Graham and a Fort Worth Cats baseball game played in their honor. By 1953 attention came from all over the country, with people calling and even stopping by Miss Babb's house to see the country's most famous old maid. The spinsters were overwhelmed and suggested that the gifts should be sent to Girlstown, U.S.A. in Whiteface, Texas. Many of the old maids knew that they would never have children of their own, so they wanted to send money to help the homeless girls instead. Girlstown was under the guidance of Miss Amelia Anthony, a fellow old maid.

Many people misunderstood the purpose of the celebration and contacted Miss Babb seeking a bride, either because they really wanted a wife or as a joke. One offer came from Cyclone Davis, who was running for governor. He sought membership in the group and described his matrimonial goals to Miss Babb in a letter. He was seeking, "the pick of your flock to sleep in Sam Houston's famous bed" in the Governor's Mansion in Austin. She was

A WBAP-TV cameraman films Miss May Marshall, the event's oldest attendee, at the reception in 1951. *From the University Photography Collection (U0458).*

Denton Mayor Mark Hannah, seated at a desk, speaks with Olive Honeycutt, one of the old maids in attendance, 1951. *From the University Photography Collection (U0458).*

'Fessor Graham oversees one of the entertainment events at an Old Maid's Day celebration, 1951. *From the University Photography Collection (U0458).*

D. Fowler (*upper left*), Honeycutt (*upper right*), Dorothy Babb (*lower left*) and Mark Hannah (*lower right*) gather behind a desk as they read over a paper. Miss Babb was described by the Dallas Morning News as "energetic, with graying hair cut in a modified poodle cut, and weighing a trim 118 pounds." *From the University Photography Collection (U0458).*

Statistics in 1953 showed that Denton had a higher than average number of old maids. The North Texas faculty alone had 92 spinsters. Miss Babb is pictured on the right in this photo from 1951. *From the University Photography Collection (U0458).*

required to be "redheaded and full of fire, with arms tapering like a swan's neck and figure like a gazelle." Apparently he wasn't successful at locating his "red headed tart" in the end.

By 1954 the event was heralded by local papers: "Hide your husbands, girls, they're coming again." That year's event began with a free screening of *Gone with the Wind* at the Interstate Theater and a personal message sent by telegram from the star, Clark Gable. The movie was followed by a tea at the Southern Hotel, emceed by 'Fessor Graham, with musical entertainment provided by musicians from NTSC including Pat Boone, then an NTSC student and up and coming musical star.

That same year Miss Babb went to Chicago to appear on a nationally televised show called "Welcome Travelers." A motorcade accompanied her to Love Field, and members of the NTSC saber drill team formed an honor guard as she got on the plane.

In 1955 Miss Babb summed up the annual event by saying, "A sure way to get women from 8 to 80 a proposal of marriage is to start an old maid's day." By that time the old maids had received letters of every kind, including letters in German or Latin, written in poetry, from servicemen in Guam, marriage offers from well-to-do bachelors and plenty from "cranks." That year Governor Allan Shivers issued a proclamation honoring the unmarried ladies of Texas and establishing August 15 as a day to honor them.

Over the years they had appeared in papers internationally, inspired sister groups all over the United States and as far away as London. They also appeared in Reader's Digest, Time and Parade. The event gradually became smaller, but the old maids still got together as late as 1965. Old Maid's Day still appears on calendars of offbeat holidays and was celebrated in 2015 on June 4.

An "unclaimed jewel" holds roses as she stands in an auditorium packed with old maids, 1951. *From the University Photography Collection (U0458).*

Women at one of the Old Maid's events in 1951 including two of the oldest ladies, sisters May and Julia Marshall of Strawn, Texas, on the right. In 1954 two prizes were given out to the oldest (Miss May Marshall, age 79) and the one from the greatest distance (Miss Lily Gulvady from India). *From the University Photography Collection (U0458).*

One of the Old Maids in attendance receives a gift at the Campus Theater, 1951. *From the University Photography Collection (U0458).*

A man pins a corsage to a woman's dress as she arrives at an Old Maid's Day event, 1951. *From the University Photography Collection (U0458).*

Several old maids sign in at one of the events, 1951. *From the University Photography Collection (U0458).*

Can You Dig It? Women Employees Can Wear Pant-Suits to Work

Once upon a time, women wore dresses and men wore pants. American women began wearing pants in the 20th century, and while women could wear pants to work in their garden, around the house or at the beach, they were still considered unprofessional for the office or school before the 1960s. That began to change during the social upheaval of the 1960s, when it became more acceptable for women to wear slacks in public. Meanwhile, hemlines for dresses and skirts rose through the 1960s to the point that in the early 1970s, fashionable women wearing miniskirts could not move naturally in or bend over in without compromising their modesty. For a period, girls would have been sent home either for wearing a short skirt or pants to school. Ankle-length skirts, called "maxi skirts" in the 1970s, could be difficult to move in, so women found pants much more practical and comfortable.

In December 1970, the *North Texas Daily* took note of the trend toward pants in an article titled "Pant-Suit Craze Overtakes Campus: Girl Watchers See Less Leg Nowadays." Men were told that they were going to have to get used to girls were wearing pants everywhere, even to "theaters, parties, school, work, in fact just about everywhere, except for church." Women's pants were seen not just stylish but also practical as well: "This is a relief for females because no girl likes to spend her entire paycheck on hosiery." In an opinion piece in the *North Texas Daily* the following year, Bettye Megason, a student, praised allowing women to wear any kind of clothing they wanted instead of following what designers in Europe told them to wear.

At the same time, the dress code for North Texas employees was evolving. In a memo with the subject "Propriety of Pants in the Office" dated January 13, 1971, the president's cabinet approved the wearing of "appropriate pantsuits" for women employees, with strict guidelines for what was considered an appropriate pantsuit. Jeans were not allowed, not were pants worn with a sweater or blouse. What it included was "loose fitting trousers" with a jacket, vest or tunic top that covered the hips and was at least as long as the wrists. They were usually dressy or tailored. Many pantsuits came in bright colors and wild patterns, but women employees were expected to be "neat and businesslike."

The controversy over women wearing pantsuits echoed much of the earlier controversy, beginning in the mid-1950s, over students wearing Bermuda shorts (knee-length tailored shorts). Though worn with long socks, male and female students had mixed feelings about the appropriateness of students wearing shorts, even during the summer heat. With air conditioning many felt that the only reason to wear shorts was to show off one's legs, and some male students felt that shorts weren't "manly" or "dignified," especially since men's knees were considered unattractive, though wearing knee socks made them a little more respectable. While some male students thought that female

Three students, including two women wearing pantsuits, on the stairs of the newly opened Willis Library, early 1970s. *From the University Photography Collection (U0458).*

Students were polled by the *Campus Chat* in 1961 and asked if wearing "more casual clothes [including Bermuda shorts] make the classroom too informal." Many students and faculty thought wearing shorts was fine, but others found them too casual for class. *Campus Chat*, June 23, 1961.

In 1956 a petition was signed by over 200 students and submitted to the student senate asking for female students to be allowed to wear shorts outside of the dorm area though still not to classes. *Campus Chat*, March 23, 1956.

Advertisement for women's pantsuits. *North Texas Daily*, September 3, 1970.

students (then called "co-eds") showing more leg was a "swell" idea, 63% thought that female students shouldn't wear shorts on campus. However, most girls felt that if the male students ("eds") wore shorts, it was only fair that they could do so as well. An op-ed piece in the 1955 *Campus Chat* suggested Bermuda shorts were quite appropriate for men, especially if worn with cable-knit socks that reached the knee, with at least a three-inch turndown of the stock. In 1956 the student senate, having received a petition with more than 200 signatures, voted to allow girls to wear shorts outside of the dorm area but not to class.

By 1961 Bermuda shorts were worn regularly by men and but by women only in special circumstances, such as on hikes or at the lake. Women were increasingly complaining about the double standard, where men had no standard dress code. The 1961 student handbook stated that "all women will want to dress appropriately at all times. Slacks and shorts are considered out of place in the living rooms and dining rooms of residence halls, campus homes and in classes." Still, social mores changed quickly: in 1962 women were wearing shorts, slacks and even jeans to sporting events and around campus. As time went on, women eventually began wearing pants to class. Originally labelled a fad, the wearing of pants and shorts by women proved it was here to stay.

Pant-Suit Craze Overtakes Campus
Girl Watchers See Less Leg Nowadays

Bermuda Poll Reveals . . .
Eds Frown on Bare Knees

DON FLY and JOY GRADICK
Poll shows students prefer this

DON FLY and JOY GRADICK
. . . instead of this.

In a 1955 poll of students, 63% believed that female students should not wear Bermuda shorts on campus, but female students overwhelmingly said that if the men were allowed to wear them, women should be allowed too. *Campus Chat,* July 29, 1955.

In December 1970 the *North Texas Daily* announced a pantsuit craze on campus. Pantsuits provided a comfortable alternative to the miniskirt, which was difficult to move in and bend over in while wearing. *North Texas Daily,* December 3, 1970.

Advertisement for women's pantsuits. *North Texas Daily,* October 13, 1970.

Bermuda Shorts Could Be Synonymous With Comfort If Men Would Cooperate

To most people, Bermuda no longer means a lush piece of geography in the Atlantic ocean, but rather a length for walking shorts averaging 11 inches at the inseam.

But at North Texas, the word "Bermuda" still means a tropical island. Why? Because the eds have been brainwashed by fat friends and piano-legged roommates into thinking it isn't proper for shorts to be worn on the campus.

Their girl friends have protested that it isn't fair for the boys to wear them when girls can't. They say they want to be comfortable too. A girl dresses to be comfortable? Not since Eve wore the fig leaf have women dressed to be comfortable. This summer they swelter through classes with three or four petticoats billowing about them. It isn't a soul-searching equation to figure out why girls want to wear shorts and why the males approve of their doing so. That isn't the problem.

The problem lies with the males and their reluctance to adopt this unbelievably comfortable hot weather wear.

One of the major complaints against the shorts is that long socks must be worn with them. These protestants must realize that the male form is not the form divine. Most men's legs are just not so graciously formed as Mamie Van Doren's. A cotton cable-stitched pair of stockings, with turn-down top, does much to improve them. The socks should come up to the kneecaps and have a three-inch turn-down.

Many of the men in this area were won over to the short pants prohibitionists by a large ad in one of the metropolitan newspapers which stated that the shorts should be worn at the beach or at home, not on the public streets or at work. Evidently the advertiser who managed to offer this sage advice did so in his air-conditioned office where he would have frozen in a pair of shorts. He couldn't have been a North Texas male who wears full-length trousers with pleasure from September through the middle of May but feels the powerful urge to molt as the thermometer approaches 85.

The idea of walking shorts is not new. Europeans have been far ahead of their more straight-laced American cousins for centuries. When thousands of American GIs went overseas and discovered this fact, they brought the idea home and it has caught on to an active market. In addition, the Air Force has adopted the short pants as regulation for summer uniforms, a practice which has been in effect for several years in the Far East.

A few simple rules should be noted here for the North Texan who chooses to be emancipated. The taller man should keep his kneecaps open to the air, but he should make sure his shorts come down as far as his kneecaps, and the hose up to them. The shorts should never be worn with short hose. A shorter Bermudan should choose shorter shorts. They will make his legs look longer.

One outstanding fashion critic set this example for the complete hot weather outfit: a pair of black poplin walking shorts, white cable stitched hose, cordovan loafers, and a jacket of English blazer cloth, blended of wool and cotton, in black with red-and-white stripings and brass buttons.

Let's face it. Walking shorts are no longer a laughing matter. The male who wears the Bermuda shorts is sure that, between his waist and his knees, is high fashion.

—Don Coppedge

A 1955 *Campus Chat* op-ed piece in encouraged men to wear Bermuda shorts. It summarized some controversial opinions about the shorts, reflecting views similar to people's feelings today about leggings. *Campus Chat,* August 5, 1955.

Literary Stars Were Once Students at North Texas

In the late 1950s North Texas was host to two bright literary talents. Prolific author Larry McMurtry and pioneering journalist Grover Lewis both graduated with B.A.s in English in 1958. The two men were friends and collaborators at North Texas, although they grew apart later in life.

As seniors at North Texas State College, McMurtry and Lewis self-published a literary journal, *Coexistence Review*, with fellow student John Lewis (no relation to Grover) as a thank-you gift for their favorite professors. The student body quickly bought out the remaining 200 copies of the print run. North Texas administrators did not approve of *Coexistence*'s mature content and reportedly threatened to investigate the authors' possible communist allegiance because of the bold red stars on the first volume's cover. As a result of the conflict, *Coexistence Review* ceased publication after two volumes. Today the surviving issues are collector's items. The controversy over *Coexistence* ultimately came to nothing, and Lewis and McMurtry graduated on time without further incident. The Special Collections department of the UNT Libraries holds both volumes of *Coexistence Review*, along with several drafts.

Larry McMurty was born June 3, 1936, in Archer City, Texas.

McMurtry contributed works of poetry, fiction and non-fiction to the campus literary magazine, *Avesta*, during his time as a student. In May 1957, during his junior year, he won $25 in an *Avesta* "best of" contest for his non-fiction essay about jazz musician Bix Beiderbecke. Reflecting on his years at North Texas in 1978, McMurty told *The North Texan* "I was quite happy here . . . I found it a very stimulating school."

After leaving North Texas, McMurtry earned an M.A. in English from Rice University in 1960. In that same year, McMurtry studied at Stanford University as a Wallace Stegner Fellow, where he befriended fellow author Ken Kesey.

McMurtry has received numerous accolades for his writing, most notably the 1986 Pulitzer Prize for Fiction for his novel *Lonesome Dove* and shared the 2006 Academy Award for Best Adapted Screenplay with Diana Ossana for *Brokeback Mountain*. McMurtry is also a three-time recipient of the Jesse H. Jones Award from the Texas Institute of Letters: in 1962 for his debut novel *Horseman, Pass By*, in 1967 for *The Last Picture Show* and in 1986 for *Lonesome Dove*. Eleven of McMurtry's novels have been adapted into motion pictures or mini-series.

In addition to his writing career, McMurtry is the longtime owner of the bookstore Booked Up in his hometown of Archer City. The original Booked Up was founded in 1971 in Washington, D.C., but moved to its current location in the Texas Panhandle in 1988. Booked Up carries over 150,000 "fine and scholarly books." McMurtry purchases and shelves all the stock himself.

McMurtry received a Distinguished Alumni Award in 1986 in recognition of his many achievements as a

What Is An Ideal University

My conception of an ideal university is admittedly somewhat radical, judged by American standards. Years ago I read a vivid description of the English system of university education which has influenced me more than anything else in forming an opinion. I am still under its spell.

I have even gone so far as to endow my ideal university with certain physical aspects. The buildings would be ancient and ivy covered, with mullioned windows. They would ~~reside~~ *sit* on hedged green lawns dotted with venerable oak trees. Somehow the ivy and the trees combine to give the school an appearance of sagacity and sobriety that would seem lacking on an ultra-modernistic campus. You feel that such a place must have fine traditions and policies, else it would not have endured so long.

I would have the faculty composed of a mixture of young and old. Men who have been mellowed by a life time of learning, teaching because of a love of knowledge and its advancement, working with men filled with youth's enthusiasm and ambition, would form a wonderful combination.

Let the student acquire an education to fit his personal needs rather than ~~tossing one at him~~ *cram one into him* which was tailored for the majority instead of the individual. I believe ~~most~~ *the average*

Is this the word you want?

Parallelism

The title page of Larry McMurtry's undergraduate essay "What Is an Ideal University," written for a course at North Texas. The instructor's comments can be seen in red. *From the Larry McMurtry Collection (RB03).*

writer. UNT again recognized his achievements at the 2014 Emerald Eagle Honors, an annual event to honor three North Texas alumni who have profoundly impacted our culture and society.

The Special Collections department holds the Larry McMurtry Collection, which contains McMurtry's undergraduate and graduate papers, correspondence and drafts of his novels *Horseman, Pass By* and *Leaving Cheyenne*. In addition, Special Collections owns first editions of McMurtry's novels in several languages, many of which are signed by McMurtry.

Grover Lewis was born November 8, 1934, in San Antonio.

As a student, Lewis won multiple awards from *The Avesta* for his short stories, non-fiction and poetry published by the magazine. Lewis was also active in North Texas' theatre scene. He was praised for his performance as Joseph Garcin in the 1957 Supper Theater production of Jean-Paul Sartre's *No Exit*. In April of that year, Lewis' original one-act play "What Rhymes with Desperation," described by *Campus Chat* reporter Vickie Massey as an "allegorical social farce depicting the uselessness of man," was staged by the Department of Drama's laboratory theater group. The following February, the Supper Theater staged another original Lewis play, "Wait for Morning, Child." The *Campus Chat* described the plot as "woven around the effects a set of false values can have on the people of a particular group." The play featured a "local-type Texas setting" in the mid-1930s. That summer the play took first place in the sixth annual National Collegiate Playwriting Contest. The prize came with a $200 award and publication by Samuel French, Inc., a notable publisher of plays. In recognition of Lewis winning the prize, North Texas State College received the 1958 Samuel French Award for "excellence in instruction in playwriting." That year, Lewis also adapted Stephen Vincent Benét's 1928 book-length narrative poem about the Civil War *John Brown's Body* for the stage. The Supper Theater held performances of *John Brown's Body* on March 27 and 28, 1958. It is possible Lewis was inspired to adapt Benét's poem by the 1953 Broadway staged reading of *John Brown* directed by Charles Laughton and starring Tyrone Power, Judith Anderson and Raymond Massey.

After graduation, Lewis spent a year teaching English in Wylie, Texas, before returning to Denton to enroll as a graduate student at North Texas. During this time Lewis supported himself as a full-time philosophy instructor at North Texas and as a book reviewer for the *Dallas Herald*. In 1960, Lewis left Denton to pursue a Ph.D. at Texas Tech in Lubbock. Lewis left Lubbock in 1963, eventually taking a post at the *Fort Worth Star-Telegram*, where he began his journalism career in earnest before moving on to the *Houston Chronicle*, *The Village Voice* and eventually his most famous post as associate editor at *Rolling Stone*. One of Lewis' best known pieces for *Rolling Stone* was "Splendor in the Short Grass," about his experience playing the part of Sonny's father in the film adaptation of McMurtry's novel *The Last Picture Show*. With this piece and others, Lewis became known as one of the forerunners of "gonzo journalism" or "New Journalism," a style of long-form literary non-fiction in which the author values "truth" over "facts."

In 1973, *Rolling Stone*'s press published a book of Lewis' poetry, *I'll Be There in the Morning If I Live*. He was working on a memoir when he died unexpectedly of lung cancer in 1995, shortly before his 61st birthday.

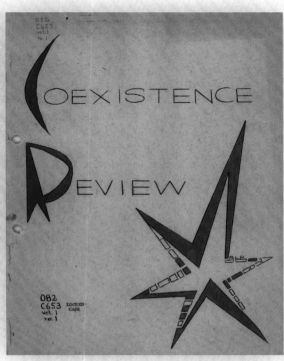

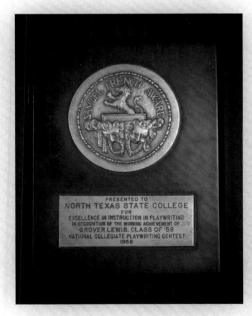

Poetry by McMurtry and Grover Lewis in *Coexistence Review*, a literary journal self-published by North Texas seniors McMurtry, Lewis and John Lewis (no relation) as a thank-you gift for some favorite professors.. *From the Larry McMurtry Collection (RB03).*

Cover of the first issue of the *Coexistence Review From the Larry McMurtry Collection (RB03).*

Plaque awarded to North Texas State College in recognition of Lewis winning the 1958 sixth annual National Collegiate Playwriting Contest for "Wait for Morning, Child."

Lewis and McMurtry receiving awards for work published in *The Avesta,* North Texas State College's literary magazine. *Campus Chat,* May 8, 1957.

"Blow the Curtain Open"

The Leon Breeden Years

While Walter Hodgson, dean of the School of Music, drafted Gene Hall to create the jazz studies program at North Texas—euphemistically referred to as "dance band"—in the late 1940s, by the late 1950s, both had left to create a similar program at Michigan State University. Replacing Hall was his good friend and former housemate, Leon Breeden.

Breeden was born in Guthrie, Oklahoma, in 1921. He directed bands at Texas Christian University while a student there, studied at the Mannes School of Music, composed large-ensemble works and arranged for the Cincinnati Pops Orchestra under Thor Johnson. Family circumstances prevented him from joining Arthur Fiedler as his chief arranger in Boston, so Breeden's next career move was directing bands at Grand Prairie High School, near Dallas, when the offer came to take over at North Texas and direct what was then the Two O'Clock Lab Band, moved to its well-known one o'clock start time shortly after Breeden took over.

The same resistance to jazz that Gene Hall faced at North Texas was waiting for Breeden. He received hate mail, late-night phone calls and warnings that he was risking his soul to eternal perdition, all leading him to compose a letter to resign after two weeks on the job. Breeden stayed on but was determined not to hand any ammunition to the program's detractors, moving pre-emptively to avoid some of the "jazzer" stereotypes among his musicians. Even goatees were forbidden in an effort to buck the stereotypes; the jazz musicians needed to surpass their peers studying traditional forms of music.

Within a few years, Breeden and Stan Kenton met at the National Stage Band Camp, beginning a long working relationship. Other successes for the One O'Clock soon followed, including a State Department-sponsored tour of Mexico in February 1967 and a concert at the White House in June of that same year, joined by Duke Ellington and Stan Getz, for President and Mrs. Lyndon B. Johnson and the king and queen of Thailand.

Breeden kept a very busy schedule. On an evening in February of 1968, when he returned exhausted from a band clinic in Louisiana, his younger son, Danny, was killed in a hit-and-run accident at the age of 19. In a scrapbook among his papers, Breeden notes on an item from the day before Danny's death: "This was my last totally happy day on this earth."

Amid such profound grief, Breeden continued working with the band in preparation for its appearance at the Music Educators' National Committee (now the National Association for Music Education) conference in Seattle

Lady Bird Johnson and the One O'Clock Lab Band, 1967. *From the Leon Breeden Collection (003).*

that March, where it performed in front of over 3,000 of America's top music educators. As they waited to play, one band member told Breeden: "Tell them not to open that curtain. We're going to blow it open in memory of your son Danny!"

Whatever prejudices about jazz the audience may have harbored before the concert, the One O'Clock obliterated them. Here was a band that was head and shoulders above many classical virtuosi and probably most of the members of the audience as well. The combination of technical proficiency, ensemble sense and emotional range of the program were such that the One O'Clock gave the first encore performance in the history of concerts at MENC conferences.

Breeden later wrote of the band's reception in his autobiography:

It was wonderful to receive letters from many parts of the United States from administrators who said in effect: "After hearing your band in Seattle, how can we get such a program started at our school?" I wrote and gave them the best advice I could, namely that it will take a strong desire on the part of many people and also must be given strong support by your administration if your program will succeed! This always reminded me that at our school we would not have survived if the desire had not been so strong on the part of all of us. I felt in summation that we succeeded in spite of and not with the help of many who could have helped us but did not.

Breeden and the One O'Clock only continued toward greater successes, playing with countless jazz legends including Ella Fitzgerald, Tony Bennett and Dizzy Gillespie. The band undertook a European tour in 1970 and in 1976 the group toured cities across the Soviet Union.

Upon Breeden's retirement, Neil Slater took over direction of the One O'Clock, and successes continued both for the band as a whole and for dozens of individual members who distinguished themselves as studio musicians, in elite jazz ensembles of the U.S. Armed Forces and in top bands like those of Stan Kenton and Maynard Ferguson. The libraries of these bands are now found in UNT's Music Library, along with Breeden's own extensive archives and the collections of other jazz greats like Willis Conover.

In a 1978 oral history, Breeden spoke of his legacy: "I have got to believe that there are some people, somewhere, that do care, and will fight for jazz education, and do realize that what we're doing, we can hold our head up and not have a jazz musician feeling that he's got to be a fourth-class citizen . . . I've gone through those put-downs my whole life, and if we can help eliminate that, my life will not have been in vain." There is no doubt that Breeden was a major force in legitimizing jazz education.

Leon Breeden, 1959. *From the Leon Breeden Collection (003).*

"The Jazz Orchestra of North Texas, USA." A Russian-language poster for the One O'Clock Lab Band's tour of the Soviet Union in June and July 1976. *From the Leon Breeden Collection (003).*

The Third Time's a Charm

Becoming Known as UNT

On May 15, 1988, UNT celebrated its long-awaited transition from North Texas State University to the University of North Texas. This would mark the seventh name for the institution since it began 125 years ago, in 1890, as the Texas Normal College and Teacher Training Institute. The event was celebrated with a small parade, the releasing of green balloons advertising the name change, the burial of a time capsule and the unveiling of both a new university seal and a brick-and-concrete sign bearing the new name.

While University Day 1988 was a festive event, it was intended "to be a joyous, but not frivolous, occasion," as achieving the new name had proved much more difficult than anticipated. After having changed names several times throughout its history, in 1961 the institution first attempted to legally change its name from North Texas State College to the University of North Texas; however, while the bill, introduced by State Representative Joe Ratcliff, easily passed the Texas House of Representatives, it met opposition in the Texas Senate from Senator Charles Herring of Austin. Because of the similarity of the proposed name, Senator Herring feared the bill would harm the University of Texas by causing confusion between the two institutions and it was reported that he claimed "it was ridiculous to think there could be two universities 'in a little town the size of Denton.'" He called North Texas State College's attempt to become the University of North Texas a "fraud on the public" and insisted that the institution "is nothing but a teachers college and that's what it's going to be for years to come." Representative Ratcliff compromised rather than let the bill die in the Senate, and the name was changed to North Texas State University.

A second attempt to change the institution's name to the University of North Texas was made during the 1969 legislative session; however, this move was once again blocked by the University of Texas at Austin. North Texas pushed for the name change again in the fall of 1986. Bills nearly died twice on the floor of the House of Representatives. The first near casualty came from Representative Wilhelmina Delco of Austin, who delayed passing the bill through the Higher Education Committee in favor of promoting her own bill. With only three days left before the end of the legislative session, the bill finally passed out of the House of Representatives committee. The second challenge for the bill came from Representative Jim Rudd of Brownfield, who, in retaliation for an unrelated slight, placed objection to five of Senator Robert J. Glasgow's bills, including that of the North Texas name change. Some quick work from members of the Calendars Committee got the bill moved to a higher priority, and the House

Governor Price Daniels signs the legislation renaming the North Texas State College into a university, May 10, 1961. *From the University Photography Collection (U0458).*

Students celebrate the first University Day with music and dancing, May 10, 1961. *From the University Photography Collection (U0458).*

A large group of students gathered for the first University Day Celebration, May 10, 1961. *From the University Photography Collection (U0458).*

An impromptu performance by North Texas band members helped rally the crowd at the first University Day, May 10, 1961. *From the University Photography Collection (U0458).*

of Representatives approved the name change. Governor Bill Clements signed the bill without any further drama or delay, officially changing the school's name effective May 15, 1988.

UNT had come a long way from its roots as a teacher's college in the upstairs rooms above a hardware store on the Courthouse Square. In the years since first trying to rename the North Texas State College, the school had increased its areas of recognized excellence from education and music to also include subjects ranging from business, journalism and public administration to library and information sciences, chemistry and computer sciences. As Chancellor Alfred F. Hurley said about the name change, "You might say a theme in the history of the institution is our aspiration to that name."

On University Day in 1988, to celebrate the newly-renamed University of North Texas, a sign bearing the new moniker was unveiled. *From the University Photography Collection (U0458).*

University officials prepare to seal the time capsule as Eppy the Eagle (the former mascot) looks on, 1988. Eppy is wearing an old NTSU jersey. *From the University Photography Collection (U0458).*

Students and faculty were given balloons carrying flyers proclaiming the final name change in 1988. The balloons were released in order to carry the name far and wide. *From the University Photography Collection (U0458).*

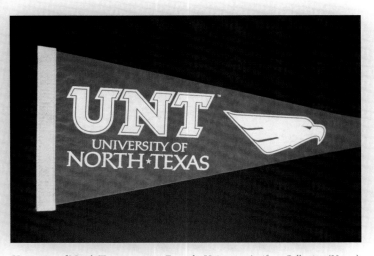

University of North Texas pennant. *From the University Artifacts Collection (U0493).*

Time Capsules Are a Blast from the Past

On April 16, 2015, the UNT community came together to celebrate our 55th annual University Day, the anniversary of the day when North Texas State College became North Texas State University.

In 1961, NTSC was ranked among the state's top institutions. At the time, NTSC enrolled more students than 16 other schools already bearing University status and was fourth in enrollment among all institutions of higher education in Texas. House Bill 645 was introduced into the Texas House of Representatives in March 1961 by NTSC alumnus Rep. Joe Ratcliff and co-signed by 8 other NTSC alumni representatives. In response, the student government engineered a letter-writing campaign in support of the bill.

Our transition from college to university became official on May 8, 1961, following the legislation's enactment. In celebration, the first University Day was held two days later. University Day is now an annual event, held in April or May to celebrate our community achieving this important milestone.

The first University Day Celebration was touted as the "biggest celebration ever." Classes were dismissed at noon, and a group of Kappa Sigma fraternity members drove a flatbed trailer onto the large slab in front of the Union Building, which then served as a commons for the campus. Cheerleaders used the flatbed as a stage to rally the crowd. The concert band performed in front of Curry Hall throughout the festivities. The celebrations culminated with a dance in the women's gymnasium, and many students attended a previously scheduled opera, "Lucia di Lammermoor," in the Auditorium Building.

In 1962, the United Students of North Texas—as the student government association was then called—documented our first year as a university in a time capsule, filling it with items that reflected the activities and concerns of the campus they served. They buried the time capsule in front of the Administration Building as a gift to the future.

A second time capsule was buried on University Day in 1988 to commemorate another significant University milestone: the seventh, and last, name change, North Texas State University became the University of North Texas.

Buried over two decades apart, the capsules had one significant similarity: both were designed to be opened on University Day, 2015. With the assistance of some impressive power tools, construction equipment and UNT Facilities staff, President Neal Smatresk unearthed both capsules, and staff of the Special Collections department of the UNT Libraries were honored to be among the first to discover what fascinating treasures hid within, and the Student Activities Center uploaded a video of the unearthing to their YouTube channel.

Mike Koury, president of the student government, and an unidentified member of the Green Jackets at the dedication of the first time capsule, May 9, 1962. *From the University Photography Collection (U0458).*

A large group gathered in front of the Administration Building for the dedication of the University's first time capsule, May 9, 1962. *From the University Photography Collection (U0458).*

Koury unveils the marker for the 1962 time capsule, buried in the flowerbed in front of the Administration Building, May 9, 1962. *From the University Photography Collection (U0458).*

Both capsules were well preserved due to the materials used to house them. The 1962 capsule alone weighed over 350 pounds! Before they were buried, the artifacts in each capsule were carefully packed into a small copper box measuring 9 × 14 × 11 inches, then cast in either limestone (1962) or steel-reinforced concrete (1988). Both boxes were buried in the flowerbed under the flagpole in front of the Hurley Administration Building.

Special Collections staff were happy to discover almost all the artifacts in the time capsule were in good condition. Due to the steel reinforcements of the 1988 box, UNT Facilities used a water jet cutter to open the encasement. A small amount of water seeped inside the box, and some of the artifacts got wet. Preservation Librarian Jessica Phillips took swift action to prevent any mold or deterioration, and the items spent the day undergoing various conservation treatments to prevent mold or other damage.

The time capsules contained a number of interesting historical artifacts, including books popular at the time they were buried.

The 1962 capsule included:

+ A copy of the 1961 yearbook, the *Yucca*
+ An audio recording of a speech given by NTSU President Mathews
+ A program from the 1962 Honors Day ceremony
+ The student handbook
+ Multiple issues of the 1962 student newspaper, the *Campus Chat*
+ Paperback editions of popular books
    o *The Catcher in the Rye* by J.D. Salinger
    o *Of Mice and Men* by John Steinbeck
    o *1984* by George Orwell
    o The Pocket Library edition of *Robert Frost's Poems*
    o *Profiles in Courage* by President John F. Kennedy

The 1988 capsule included:

+ A copy of the 1988 yearbook, the *Aerie*
+ A 1962 male NTSU Cheerleader uniform complete with a green and white pompom
+ A video message from President Hurley to be viewed by the UNT Chancellor in 2015
+ Multiple issues of the 1988 student newspaper, the *North Texas Daily*
+ Memorabilia from campus blood drive activities: shirts, buttons, vampire teeth and stickers
+ Paperback editions of popular books (donated by Paul Voertman)

The 1962 time capsule was a sealed copper box. Buried underground for over 50 years, it held up rather well! *From the 1962 North Texas State University Time Capsule Collection (U0587).*

Students included a number of popular paperbacks in the 1962 time capsule. *From the 1962 North Texas State University Time Capsule Collection (U0587).*

The 1962 time capsule included an audio recording of the championship debate between the newly renamed North Texas State University Debate Team against the University of Florida. *From the 1962 North Texas State University Time Capsule Collection (U0587).*

- *Bright Lights Big City* by Jay McInerney
- *Lonesome Dove* by North Texas alumnus Larry McMurtry
- *The Closing of the American Mind* by Allan Bloom
- A color portrait of the 1988 NTSU Drumline and a sheet with the members' contact info

The artifacts in the time capsule are now held by the Special Collections department of the UNT Libraries.

Many of the members of the 1988 NTSU Drumline have gone on to prolific music careers. Do you recognize any names or faces? *From the 1988 Time Capsule Collection (U0587).*

The 1988 time capsule included a video-recorded message of President Hurley's address to the future chancellor of the University of North Texas. The full video has been digitized and made available in the UNT Digital Library. *From the 1988 Time Capsule Collection (U0587).*

Merrill Ellis

Electronic Music Pioneer

Merrill Ellis' story at North Texas echoes many recurring themes in the 125-year history of the university: humble beginnings, ingenuity and innovation. The Electronic Music Center he founded in 1963 in a house at 1721 Mulberry Street (near Avenue D) laid the foundation for what is now the Center for Experimental Music and Intermedia (CEMI) in the College of Music's Division of Composition Studies.

Born in 1916 in Cleburne, Texas, Ellis studied clarinet as a child and earned a bachelor's degree in 1939 and a master's degree in 1941, both from the University of Oklahoma. He also studied composition privately with Roy Harris, Spencer Norton, Charles Garland and Darius Milhaud. He joined the North Texas faculty in 1962 after teaching band, orchestra and choir in high schools in Texas and Missouri and a variety of subjects including music education and music theory at several colleges in Missouri. At North Texas, Ellis taught music theory and composition in addition to directing the Electronic Music Center. During the 1960s, Ellis persuaded Robert Moog to build a synthesizer—the second "Moog" ever made—for North Texas.

A prolific composer, Ellis' own works spanned a wide range of instrumentation with and without electronic components. In 1975, he received an award from the Association of Composers, Authors and Publishers (ASCAP) for the ninth consecutive year for his contributions to "serious" music.

The Electronic Music Center grew in stature under Ellis; a new Intermedia Theater was established in 1979 and now bears his name. Ellis, who died in 1981, was succeeded as director by Larry Austin and Phil Winsor, who continued to raise the profile of the center, particularly at the 1981 International Computer Music Conference (ICMC), when 400 scientists and composers of computer music, including guest composers John Cage and Lejaren Hiller, visited North Texas.

The EMC was renamed the Center for Experimental Music and Intermedia (CEMI) in 1983, reflecting the expanded scope of activities growing out of Ellis' leadership. Martin Mailman, a fellow composer and longtime member of the College of Music faculty, said in 1986:

> *Merrill was a valued colleague and friend who was a true pioneer in electronic and multimedia music. His works express, far more eloquently than any words of mine could, his unique contribution to the music of our time. Indeed, his creative vision was a cornerstone in the establishment of CEMI. It has been a privilege to have an opportunity to celebrate his memory in this environment that he inspired with his work and spirit.*

The Music Library and Special Collections department of the UNT Libraries each hold collections from Ellis. The Music Library's collection includes a variety of performance materials for his works: tapes, cassettes, slides, films and instructions, along with a lecture by John Cage. UNT Special Collections holds photographs, correspondence and other documents related to Ellis' life and career. Both are available for use by special arrangement with their respective departments.

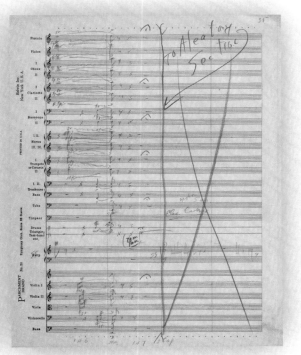

Merrill Ellis and the second ever "moog" (synthesizer designed by Robert Moog), built for use at North Texas, 1960s. *From the Merrill Ellis Collection (UG.23).*

A page from the manuscript score of Ellis' 1969 composition "Kaleidoscope." *From the Merrill Ellis Collection (UG.23).*

Ellis, 1970s. *From the University Photography Collection (U0458).*

Charles Dickens in Denton

The Vann Victorian Collection

The Special Collections department of the UNT Libraries holds over 20,000 cataloged publications ranging from 15th-century printed books to modern first editions. Included in this vast trove is the Vann Victorian Collection, a treasure of the UNT Libraries and an exceptional resource for the study of Victorian literature. Materials in the collection include 19th-century British fiction, poetry and original periodicals.

Charles Dickens is perhaps the best known writer of the Victorian era. His work vividly portrays the changes in British society during the 19th century, when rapid industrialization and urbanization resulted in high unemployment and housing shortages, forcing many people into the deplorable conditions of tenement homes. It was in this atmosphere that a young Charles Dickens grew up, in a slum he described as "as shabby, dingy, damp, and mean a neighbourhood, as one would desire not to see." The experiences of Dickens' childhood left him with a lifelong concern for the most helpless and neglected members of society and provided him with inspiration for his novels. Dickens especially had sympathy for children, whom he compassionately portrayed again and again in characters like Tiny Tim Cratchit, David Copperfield and Oliver Twist.

Highlights of the Vann Victorian Collection include a first edition of Charles Dickens' *A Christmas Carol*, a full run of the periodical *All the Year Round* (which published the first serialization of *A Tale of Two Cities*) and other serialized first editions of Dickens' works, including *Our Mutual Friend*, *Bleak House* and *David Copperfield*. The Vann Victorian collection also includes important first editions of the works of other Victorian writers such as Alfred Lord Tennyson, William Makepeace Thackeray, Matthew Arnold and Augustus Mayhew.

Charles Dickens is also known for pioneering a new method of book publication. Beginning with his first novel, *The Posthumous Papers of the Pickwick Club*, Dickens used a "part issue" format, with each part containing thirty-two pages of text with two engraved illustrations bound in green paper. There were twenty monthly parts, each appearing on the last day of the month, with the last part a double issue containing both parts XIX and XX. Each part contained several pages of advertisements. The last part contained a title page, preface, dedication and table of contents, so the purchaser could take the entire set to a binder and have it made into a bound volume.

Until Dickens began publishing, the part issue had been used almost exclusively for reprinting popular works such as encyclopedias and the Bible. Nine of his novels were published in this format, with the unfinished work *The*

Don and Dolores Vann in their home in Denton, 2014.

Dickens, Charles. *A Christmas Carol: In Prose: Being a Ghost Story of Christmas.* Illus. John Leech. London, 1844 (PR4572 .C68 1844).

Forster, John. *The Life of Charles Dickens.* London, 1900 (PR4581 .F7 1900z).

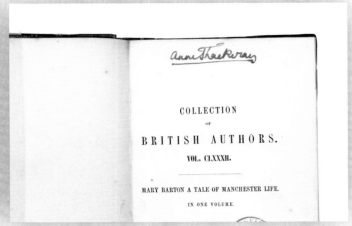

Gaskell, Elizabeth C. *Mary Barton: A Tale of Manchester Life.* Leipzig, 1849 (PR4710 .M3 1849). This volume belonged to Anne Thackeray (1837–1919), whose initials "A.I.P" are found gilt-stamped into the first spine compartment from the head and whose signature appears at the top of the title page. The eldest daughter of the novelist William Makepeace Thackeray, Anne was a lifelong friend of the Dickens children.

Mystery of Edwin Drood projected for twelve parts. Six other novels by Dickens were first published in magazines and were later offered for sale as bound volumes.

J. Don Vann, Regents Professor Emeritus of English, and his wife Dolores, after whom the Victorian collection at UNT is named, generously donated many important first editions. Vann joined the faculty of UNT in 1964, teaching courses on Victorian literature. His doctoral dissertation on the critical reception of David Copperfield in London newspapers led him to be a founding member of the Research Society for Victorian Periodicals.

Having been members of the London Dickens Fellowship for many years, the Vanns founded the Denton Dickens Fellowship in 1987. The branch received a charter from the international Dickens Fellowship the following year. On two occasions Professor Vann was given the honor of delivering the eulogy at the annual wreath-laying ceremony at Dickens' grave in Poet's Corner in Westminster Abbey.

In 2004 the Vanns established the Vann Victorian Endowment to provide a permanent fund to purchase Victorian books for the Vann Victorian Collection at UNT.

Dickens, Charles. *Our Mutual Friend*. Illus. Marcus Stone. London, 1865 (PR4568 .A1 1865). *Our Mutual Friend* was Dickens fourteenth novel, published in parts from May 1864 to November 1865. The novel is a parable of the corruption brought by money.

An assortment of first edition works by Alfred Lord Tennyson.

The Vanns dressed in Victorian attire, year unknown. *From the Dr. J. Don Vann Manuscript Collection (AR0809).*

The UNT Oral History Program

In 1965 the UNT Oral History Program was founded to capture the stories of the "man on the street" in their own words, giving voice to those often neglected by history because they are less likely to leave a written record. The goal of the program is to "preserve, through recorded interviews, the memoirs of Texans who have been eyewitnesses to or participants in historic events," and to make transcripts of these oral interviews available to scholars and the general public. The program celebrated its 50th anniversary in 2015 by posting audio clips and photos highlighting important portions of the collection, one of the nation's largest and oldest.

It all began in 1964 when H.W. Decamp, a faculty member in political science, called a meeting with the intention of establishing a program to preserve the recollections of Texas politicians and business leaders. By 1968 the leadership was taken over Ronald E. Marcello, a history professor, who started expanding beyond the original scope to include those who served in World War II, participants in New Deal programs and Holocaust survivors. Marcello led the program till 2005, when Todd Moye, another history professor, took over, continuing to expand the scope of the collection.

As of 2015 the collection includes more than 1,800 oral histories consisting of yielding 150,000 pages of transcribed oral interviews from an expanded focus that now includes local African American, entrepreneurial, LGBTQ, women's and community history.

The collection includes interviews with prominent political figures, such as Judge Sarah T. Hughes, who served as a federal district judge in 1961 and swore in Lyndon Johnson after the Kennedy assassination, becoming the first woman to swear in a president. Senator Barbara Jordan, who served as the first African-American member of the Texas legislature since Reconstruction, talks about her experiences as a senator along with her comments about Martin Luther King, Malcolm X, the Black Panthers and other important African-Americans during the 1960s in a 1970 interview. The LGBTQ community has increasingly becoming an important part of the collection. Cece Cox, the CEO of the Resource Center, discusses her work as an advocate in the LGBTQ community in Dallas for more than thirty years in a 2012 oral history.

Interviews from the Civil Rights movement also form an important part of the collection. These include interviews with residents of Quakertown, in Denton, who were forcibly evicted to the southeast part of town in the early 1920s, and the recollections of Joe Atkins, the African American man whose lawsuit in 1955 brought about the desegregation of UNT. Joba Ramirez talks about her experience as a member of the Mexican-American community in Denton and her parent's efforts to integrate her family into the local Anglo community.

This panoramic group photograph of members of the Pineland Civilian Conservation Corps camp in 1933 shows a typical CCC camp as described in reminiscences captured by the UNT Oral History Program. *From the Connie Ford McCann Civilian Conservation Corps Collection (AR0240).*

President J.C. Matthews shown in 1965 in what is now the Eagle Commons Library talking to a teleprinter operator. The teleprinter was a special type of typewriter used to send messages over various communication channels in the days before computers. Matthews was interviewed in 1977 and 1984. *From the University Photography Collection (U0458).*

A tent crew pose with their cleaning supplies for a photograph in Pineland, Texas. *From the Connie Ford McCann Civilian Conservation Corps Collection (AR0240).*

James Carl Matthews, president of North Texas from 1951 to 1968, was interviewed in 1977 and 1984 about his experiences implementing desegregation from 1954 to 1956 and his recollection of the attitude and opinions of everyone involved. He reflected on incidents at the Campus Theatre, the desegregation of local businesses and the athletic program.

Entrepreneurial and business interviews in the collection include the oral histories of Mary Kay Ash, founder of Mary Kay Cosmetics, and her son Richard Rogers, who served as president of Mary Kay Cosmetics. In their 1974 interviews, they discuss Ash's business philosophy, the role of women in her company and the reasons for the growth of the company.

The collection also includes interviews with longtime Denton businessmen Tom Harpool and Paul Voertman, who gave insights into business practices in Denton from the early 20th century. Harpool was interviewed in 1982 about his family background, move to Denton in 1928, his employment at the North Texas State Teacher's College Book Bindery, the Depression and his social and civic activities. He eventually purchased a cotton, grain and seed business in Denton, and his interview discusses local agricultural and business practices including raising livestock in Denton and the use of chemicals such as DDT. Voertman, the president of Voertman's Book Store, was interviewed about the founding of the store by his father, Roy Voertman, in 1925. In his 1977 interview, he discussed the early years of store, the great Depression, his education at North Texas and the University of Texas and his work experience.

Military history and interviews of men in the Civilian Conservation Corps (CCC), a New Deal work-relief program, have long been a highlight of the collection. Fascinating oral histories from CCC participants are complemented by an assemblage of World War II reminiscences from prisoners of war, participants in the air offensive in Europe and the Pacific naval war, Pearl Harbor survivors, and Holocaust survivors. Men such as Charles Lindberg, a World War II marine veteran, shared his memories of his service in the Pacific Theater and how the war has been remembered.

Oral histories from the UNT Oral History Program are available for use by scholars, students, genealogists and anyone with an interest in history.

Charles Edward "Joe" Greene (*second from left*), a famed North Texas football player, at an alumni banquet, 1976. Standing with Greene are, left to right, Tom Harpool, president of the UNT Alumni Association, and distinguished alumni Chester A. Newland and Larry A. Jobe. Harpool was interviewed by the UNT Oral History Program in 1982 about his life and business practices in Denton from the 1920s to the 1980s. *From the University Photography Collection (U0458).*

Marcello sits at a table on the third floor of Willis Library demonstrating the use of reel-to-reel recording equipment, 1975. *From the University Photography Collection (U0458).*

Ronald Marcello (left), longtime director of the UNT Oral History Program, with Texas Senator Oscar Mauzy (second from the right) and President Frank E. Vandiver (right) celebrating the completion of the 500th oral history added to the collection in 1981. The collection includes twelve interviews with Senator Mauzy discussing his role in the 60th through 68th Texas Legislatures. *From the University Photography Collection (U0458).*

Stay Tuned to KNTU!

Hello out there in radio land! In the spotlight today, it's the smooth sounds of KNTU, FM 88.1. On the agenda, a bit of history for you.

Did you know our university radio station was started many moons ago on Halloween of '69? With an FCC license in hand and broadcasting 440 watts, students' dream of a real radio station was realized on that day. The first program aired was Orson Wells' *War of the Worlds*. Bill Mercer, the voice of the Eagles during basketball and football seasons, became the first station manager.

After coming to North Texas to work on his master's degree, Mercer was approached by Reg Holland, chair of the speech and drama program, who hoped to persuade him to teach communication classes. He agreed, and these communication classes would become the foundation for a campus radio station.

Mercer prepared himself and 100 communications students for the birth of KNTU, staging mock radio station productions and programming in what is now Curry Hall. It was a daunting task to get the station on its feet. Even getting call letters seemed to be a problem. During the preliminary planning, it was discovered that the call letters KNTU were assigned to a Coast Guard cutter ship, located in a dry dock on the Atlantic coast. But with a little back and forth, NT was granted the call letters, and KNTU was born.

All those years ago, on the Halloween of '69, there was a grand opening ceremony for the station, with many North Texas students and the president in attendance. Everyone in the station was a bit nervous, and understandably so. When it came time to switch the on-air light on, the student at the audio console hit the button, but the music came out at the wrong speed! Frantic and trying to set the speed right, he let out a loud curse word, heard only by Mercer and early listeners. What's Halloween without an on-air expletive? With that, KNTU was live.

In the beginning, the station was run by 10 people, including Mercer, broadcasting from noon till 7 p.m. Much of the music played during the DJ's timeslots was their own. It was only a matter of time before the station amassed its private music library for on-air use. As Mercer said about those early years, the station "had a lot of tapes, but few people." Programming was often syndicated and included talk shows, dramas and music programs.

One of the first procedures instituted by Mercer was the play clock. DJs had to follow the play clock to the tee, or Mercer would call in from his home in Richardson and get things back on schedule. He was preparing his students for professional radio and would tell them outright if they couldn't follow format, he would find someone who could!

Bruce Jackson, Steve Negion and Ted Colson, three DJs at KNTU, during a show, circa 1970s. *From the University Photography Collection (U0458).*

A KNTU disc jockey retrieves a vinyl record to play during his set, undated. *From the University Photography Collection (U0458).*

Exterior of Smith Hall, undated. *From the University Photography Collection (U0458).*

With the 1970s came new live morning programming and two radio personalities who would go on to carve out their own paths in the media. Gary Brobst and Doug Adams, two of Mercer's students assigned the morning show project, took knowledge and experience gained at the station with them to their current positions. Brobst became vice president of EZ Communications in Phoenix, while Adams went on to become President and General Manager of KXAS / NBC 5 in Fort Worth.

In 1980–1981, the station expanded its programming to 365 days a year, with its audience growing beyond Denton thanks to the powerhouse wattage increase to 6700 watts, blasting the airwaves with Mean Green pride. Though the station grew formidably in the early 1980s, it was in the 1984–1985 school year that KNTU moved to Smith Hall and began to emerge as the station it is today. By 1988, KNTU was broadcasting an explosive 100,000 watts.

Disaster struck on June 22, 1989, a fire ravaged Smith Hall. Almost all of the audio equipment and albums were destroyed, and only 200 of the 250 newly acquired CDs remained intact.

To keep the play clock ticking, KNTU moved into the Historical Building (now Curry Hall). With the help of a grant from the Texas legislature, KNTU rebuilt its station in Smith Hall, moving back into their previous home in May 1990. In April of 2001, KNTU moved into their newly renovated suite in the RTVF building shortly before Smith hall was razed.

To this day, KNTU continues to be a powerhouse station. Not only does it provide radio and communications majors with hands-on studio experience, it also provides Denton and the North Texas region with amazing programming. As Mercer once said about the station's early years: "It was a building time, a learning time, a wild time . . . We had a ball." KNTU continues to do just that.

A KNTU disc jockey reaches for the vinyl record to play on-air, undated. *From the University Photography Collection (U0458).*

Groovy Students Attend the Texas International Pop Festival

Two weeks after the Woodstock Music Festival in New York, another history-making concert, the Texas International Pop Festival, took place over three days in Lewisville, Texas. Over Labor Day Weekend in 1969, over 100,000 people converged on a site located a short distance from Denton at I-35 and Round Grove Road near Lake Lewisville to hear some of top performing artists of the day, including Janis Joplin, Led Zeppelin and B.B. King.

Students at North Texas were among the attendees who were described in newspaper accounts as "hippies," "flower children," and "long hairs." Advertisements in the student newspaper, the *Campus Chat*, advertised advance ticket sales for $6 per day. Bob Anderson, a reporter for the *Campus Chat* who wrote about his experience at the festival, said he made the thirty-minute drive from Denton each day to experience the festivities, although some fellow students took advantage of free camping provided by the festival organizers.

In his *Campus Chat* article on September 19, 1969, Anderson said that the "the most controversial aspects of the gathering were the free use and sale of drugs inside the festival area and nude swimming at various campsites." The *Dallas Morning News* reported that Lewisville Police had reached an agreement with festival promoters and "hippie leaders" to refrain from making arrests inside the festival grounds and would rely on "self-policing" to maintain order. An informal police force composed of festival goers was established inside the festival grounds. An August 30, 1969, a *Dallas Morning News* article described one colorful "policeman" as wearing a Robin Hood cap, with long hair, a beard and a necklace made of teeth.

Music on the main festival stage was scheduled to begin each day at 4:30 p.m. and continued long into the night. Concert goers created bootleg recordings of some acts, including an hour-long, seven-song set performed by Led Zeppelin on August 31, 1969. Recordings of performances be Janis Joplin and Grand Funk Railroad recorded at the festival are now widely available.

The UNT Oral History Collection contains several interviews with attendees who describe performances. For example, Harold Corey, a high school student in Dallas at the time of the festival, remembers seeing Janis Joplin perform, saying "the thing that stands out in my mind more than anything about her was that during the whole concert she had a fifth of Jack Daniels in her hand and was chugging it straight out of the bottle throughout the whole concert."

An advertisement listing the musical acts performing at the Texas International Pop Festival. *Appendix to Oral History 1527.*

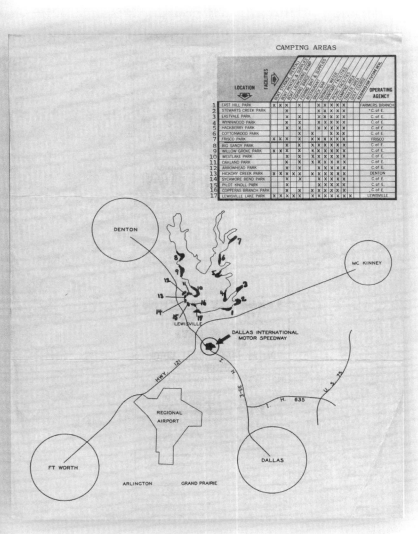

Map and directions to the Texas International Pop Festival, 1969. *Appendix to Oral History 1527.*

The Texas International Pop Festival helped to solidify an already growing music scene in the North Texas region. In another oral history, Randell Fields discusses the long-term impact of the festival. Fields, who attended the festival as a high-school student, said, "that festival . . . legitimized a lot of the music community here in Dallas . . . a lot of the bands that came here and experienced that festival understood that there was an audience for them." UNT and the Denton community continue that tradition today by supporting a rich and diverse music scene, which includes many annual music festivals.

The Texas Historical Commission placed a marker in Lewisville in 2010 to commemorate the festival, citing its importance as an introduction for many citizens to changing cultural norms in the North Texas region. The marker is located in the 900 block of Lakeside Circle, near the Hebron Station of the A-train.

Campus Chat staff, 1969. *From the University Photography Collection (U0458).*

Campus Chat reporter Bob Anderson, 1969. *From the University Photography Collection (U0458).*

Anderson, Bob. "Old Pop Festivals Never Die; The Smoke Just Fades Away." *Campus Chat,* September 16, 1969.

LGBT Life

Living and Learning at UNT

The Denton Gay Alliance (DGA) was established in 1975 under the leadership of North Texas student Ruben Salinas. On March 12, 1976 Salinas asked President C. C. Nolen's cabinet to formally recognize DGA as a campus organization. The Cabinet denied the request on March 23 because DGA was partially composed of non-student members, a barrier to official recognition. The DGA operated as a campus social chapter for a few more years but fizzled out after Salinas graduated and left Denton.

In October 1976 a North Texas student calling himself "MWF" wrote a series of letters to *North Texas Daily* editor Terry Pair about his life as an out gay man. MWF's letters captured a young man struggling with his sexuality and public identity. The anonymous author admitted he'd contemplated suicide and closed one letter with "Don't tell me about the well-adjusted gay." DGA and an unidentified gay professor responded to MWF's letters in the November 24 issue of the *North Texas Daily* to encourage MWF and other "maladjusted homosexuals" to seek help. The DGA used their editorial to rebut the president's cabinet's refusal to formally recognize the DGA earlier in the year. Identifying MWF as "the kind of person the [DGA] was formed to help, but has been unable to reach," the DGA authors encouraged the university administration to re-read the letters by MWF, claiming MWF's "case is a perfect example of why the DGA is needed at NTSU." A final round of despondent letters by MWF (apparently written well before the editorials in response) were published in the December 1 *North Texas Daily*. In this issue, Pair suggests that MWF might have been a prank but acknowledges that "nobody in our culture" understands "how gays can blend into American society."

The first meeting of the Gay/Lesbian Association of Denton (GLAD) was held August 29, 1979, in a private home. The attendance at the first meeting was a modest seven people but soon as many as 200 people were attending events advertised in the "Notepad" section of the *Denton-Record Chronicle*.

Today the predominant campus organization for students who identify as gay, lesbian, bisexual, transgendered or otherwise queer is GLAD: UNT's Queer Alliance. The organization, whose website claims a membership of 300, maintains Facebook and Tumblr pages, along with Instagram and Twitter accounts. On October 10, 2014, GLAD celebrated National Coming Out Day (nationally observed on October 11) by asking the campus community to sign a door installed temporarily on the Library Mall.

Nuntius Float in the First Gay Pride Parade in Dallas. *From the Resource Center LGBT Collection (AR0756).*

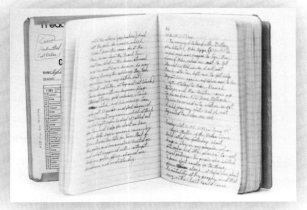

On October 26, 1991, Hugh Callaway and his partner Thanh Nguyen were attacked in Reverchon Park in Dallas. Nguyen was killed. Callaway's journal documents the crime, as well as his frustrations with police as the murder suspect was brought to trial. *From the Resource Center LGBT Collection (AR0756).*

Terry Pair
'MWF' Letters Give Homosexual Insights

Dear Editor,

Ever since I have attended college I have run across several articles, letters to the editor and the like that have all dealt with the question of being gay. I have read them enough, and I think it's time someone else told about the other side.

I'm 21-years-old and have been involved in the gay life since I was 17 or 18. Before I "came out" I often heard or read secretly about what it meant to "be a homosexual," but, of course, you can never know until you experience it.

There are some things, though, that those books never tell you. What about the loneliness or the sneers if someone finds out? Or the fear that parents or special friends will find out.

I know that the enlightened gay would quickly shoot a rebuttal in my direction. I don't really care. I've had worse experiences.

I'll write again when I have the nerve. Whether you like it or not, you're my place I can sound off.

No Name, MWF

On Oct. 20, the letter above disrupted the seemingly nonstop routine of my job. It was a total surprise and a mystery. Was it for real? Was it a joke? And, either way, what was its purpose?

I kept the puzzle to myself.

The next day, I received two more letters from "MWF." One had been typed on a different typewriter than the first letter. The back side of it was covered with penned scrawlings—a brief indication

that a cassette recording was on the way, an old Aggie joke.

THE TYPED section took the words out of my mouth. It read: "Are you surprised to get another letter so soon? I'm kind of surprised myself. This doesn't fit my style at all."

I hadn't developed a style for receiving letters from strangers. But the rest of the letter fascinated me.

MWF said he does not fit the gay stereotype, saying that no one suspects him of being a gay except for those who already know.

"To begin with," MWF wrote in his mockery of the gay stereotype, "I have about a 3.7 or 3.8 GPA. Are you impressed? I didn't think you would be. I also am interested in tennis and football, along with other sports. The only kind of sports gays are supposed to be interested in are indoor."

His humor disappeared without any indication of his thought transition. MWF said there is no such thing as a well-adjusted homosexual. He said he had considered killing himself. But he can't give up his lifestyle.

He talked about insecurity and marriage for security's sake. Then he cut the letter short.

THE NEXT day I received another letter, this one addressed to "Terry" instead of "Editor." The "personalized" letter was a sequel to the last one, a detailed look at the insecurity that plagues the gays who make the Dallas "cruise scene."

He listed Main and Houston in Fort Worth and Oaklawn in Dallas as the places to shop. With enough cruising, MWF wrote, the gay develops a sixth sense for knowing who is gay and who isn't.

"...but I want to tell you about...the park. There is a park in Dallas (any self-respecting gay will know what it is) where gay sex is a fairly easy thing to come by," he wrote. "Depending on how aggressive you tend to be, you can pick gays up without really killing yourself or wasting gas like you do when you cruise."

He continued, describing what kind of dress does the trick and what to say when approached by an attractive or unattractive prospect.

After a page-and-a-half of dry, sardonic description, he closed with: "Don't tell me about the well-adjusted gay."

Letters to the editor in response to letter by MWF, North Texas Daily, November 24, 1976.

ndicapped
oblems

Finding out what is on a menu and opening his post office box can be challenges.

"Sometimes it's hard to find out what's for lunch when I come over here (University Union)," he said. "And some of the post office boxes are hard to open. I need someone to help me open mine."

Of the 168 handicapped students at NTSU, however, only 33 have asked the university through

Feedback
Gays Reply to MWF Letter

The Denton Gay Alliance

MWF requested in one of his letters to you not to be told about the well-adjusted gay. Fine, we won't tell him. Instead, we will tell him about the maladjusted homosexual.

MWF is a prime example of such a person, who allows himself, through his own fears and inhibitions, to be victimized and conditioned by the antihomosexual society that he lives in. He is the kind of person the Denton Gay Alliance (DGA) was formed to help, but has been unable to reach. MWF manifests a very negative 1960s "Boys in the Band" type of attitude towards his homosexuality.

The NT administration and Board of Regents should take another long look at the MWF article. His case is a perfect example of why the DGA is needed at NTSU.

Now is the time for the gay population of NTSU to reevaluate their thoughts and to regroup to assure that recent court decisions throughout the nation do not set precedent and begin a trend toward the annihilation of still another minority in the "melting pot" of the world.

Gay Prof Calls MWF 'Tragic'

It is to your credit that you recognize the tragedy implicit in the letters you received from "MWF." However, there is a deeper tragedy about this attitude which I doubt you or your readers realize. There are "well-adjusted" gays, but MWF doesn't know who they are, nor do they know his identity to help him, because neither he nor they dare reveal their sexual orientation to others.

I know, for I am one myself, a faculty member who might even have had MWF in class—but neither of us would have guessed. Nor would he probably guess about most of my friends. For instance, I know three male couples who have lived together from 20 to 30 years. They all hold good professional jobs, have beautiful homes to which their colleagues are never invited, and are respected by society. The oldest pair, about to retire, and the 20-year couple are faithful to each other; the other two live in a more open way but have so much in common that neither they nor their friends and relatives (who know) could imagine them apart. One doesn't find this kind of person in the bars; one never finds them at home. And unless one is very lucky, one never finds one of us and, and, like MWF, hates oneself because the only role models one has are those

who have nothing to lose, or who are desperate enough they don't care if they do lose what they have.

The situation is changing. In recent years—even months—figures in the arts and entertainment have come out into the open. Many professional organizations have established gay groups within them. A few sympathetic treatments have appeared on T.V. The Denton Record Chronicle last week carried a sympathetic article on Mary Jo Risher—a "well-adjusted" gay who has lost much through having her sexual preferences known. Perhaps someday soon the faculty and administrators will begin daring to speak and to help students by showing that all gays are not worthless.

Brienza Offers 'Perspective'
Bill Brienza
101 McConnell Hall

No Mr. Kruse, I have not gone to Ceylon, India or Red China where freedom of the press does not exist, I have decided to stay at NTSU where freedom of the press is often irresponsible.

Ralph Winingham's editorial of Nov. 18, puts the question of freedom of the press in a nutshell, but only from The Daily's perspective. Withholding information from The Daily is far from criminal; while it may be a shame, it is very justifiable. As one who has been misquoted or quoted out of context too many times in the past, I cannot find fault with Vice-President of Student Affairs Jane Smith or any other university official for refusing to comment on "news" stories.

The Daily's sophomore reporters are notorious for inaccuracy, and the paper itself editorializes its "news" stories. Headlines are catchy but misleading. Incomplete reporting is convention with The Daily. If all the facts cannot fit within the alloted colum space, they do not get printed. I have been here for four years and never have I seen a "continued-on-page-3" news story.

Anyone who trusts The Daily to report honestly and fairly is a fool, and Mrs. Smith, thank God, is no fool. Because The Daily uses the innuendo so expertly, the innocent suffer with the guilty. I am sure Mrs. Smith is acting in the interest of the innocent and this university when she refuses comment on this alleged incident. When The Daily can promise complete exposure without character assassination, when it can get all the facts straight, and reform itself from its yellow-journalism tendencies, then maybe The Daily will be rehabilitated.

Until then Mr. Winingham, you'll just have to suffer from the pitfall of your vocation—lack of trust.

Grand Jury Ir Pot-Smugglir

RIO GRANDE CITY (AP)—"We wouldn't mind the smuggling, if they'd just pay taxes on it," joked a Starr County resident.

The smuggling involves an estimated 20,000 to 40,000 pounds of marijuana a week, brought from Mexico across the willow-lined Rio Grande into the brush of this South Texas county for distribution in northern cities.

It is the work of the "mafiosos" and a thriving "family" business in this county of 17,000 people, according to state and county investigators working with a grand jury currently probing the smuggling activity.

"Mafiosos" is a word used in northern Mexico to describe those involved in marijuana or heroin smuggling.

Law enforcement officers say the identities of the criminals are known to many residents of the area on both sides of the border, but fear of involvement and physical harm plus a distrust of law-enforcement agencies have made investigation difficult.

"I'D SAY there are at least 10 major families involved and when I say major families, I mean big

Letters to the editor in response to letter by MWF, North Texas Daily, November 24, 1976.

On October 11, 2013, UNT opened the Pride Alliance, a resource and training center for members of the LGBTIQA community and their allies. On the occasion of the Pride Alliance's opening, vice president for institutional equity and diversity Gilda Garcia said, "All of us can take pride in the fact that this will be the first time UNT has a university-sponsored, designated meeting place for LGBT community members."

UNT offers an interdisciplinary 18-credit-hour LGBT Studies undergraduate minor, currently directed by Mark Vosvick, professor of psychology, for UNT students interested in studying the intersection of sexuality, gender, culture, politics and society. UNT is the first university in the North Texas region to offer an undergraduate minor in LGBT studies.

The Special Collections department of the UNT Libraries is currently focused on acquiring archival collections to support the increased interest on campus in the study of LGBT history. In fall 2012, Special Collections received the Resource Center LGBT Collection, an archival collection documenting over 60 years of LGBT life and activism in the North Texas region. The Resource Center LGBT Collection complements similar collections of historical materials in San Francisco, Los Angeles and New York City. The heart of the collection originates from gay activist Phil Johnson's personal archive of LGBT artifacts, media and publications, which Johnson donated to the Resource Center in 1994. In 2013, the UNT Libraries acquired an interrelated series of personal collections created by members of The Dallas Way, a nonprofit organization founded in 2011 by Jack Evans and George Harris that is dedicated to gathering, storing, organizing and presenting the complete history of Dallas' gay, lesbian, bisexual and transgender community.

With any luck, now that UNT is better equipped to support LGBTIQA students and the study of gender and sexuality, no UNT student will again feel the despair and isolation expressed by MWF in 1976.

A student views materials from the Resource Center LGBT Collection at a 2013 exhibit at Willis Library. *From the Junebug Clark University Photo Collection (AR0814).*

Morgan Gieringer (*second from left*), head of special collections, shows Deborah Leliaert, vice president for university relations, communications and marketing (*left*), an exhibit on the Resource Center LGBT Collection, October 17, 2013. *From the Junebug Clark University Photo Collection (AR0814).*

Dallas Gay Alliance t-shirt. *From the Resource Center LGBT Collection (AR0756).*

Dave Lewis and Bill Nelson at Pride III. *From the Resource Center LGBT Collection (AR0756).*

Associate Dean of Libraries Cathy Hartman (*left*), activist Phil Johnson (*center*) and Ph.D. student Karen Wisely (*right*) at a reception for opening of the exhibit on the Resource Center LGBT Collection, October 17, 2013. *From the Junebug Clark University Photo Collection (AR0814).*

Clubbing on Campus at the Rock Bottom Lounge

The Rock Bottom Lounge opened in the North Texas State University Union in 1976 as a restaurant and nightclub for university students. Featuring a nightly happy hour, which included beer, wine and a full dinner menu, students gathered nightly to enjoy live music from local acts, including UNT music students in the jazz lab bands.

On-campus pubs were common in colleges and universities throughout the 1970s and 1980s. The legal drinking age in most states was 18 or 19 during this time, and pubs on campus provided a place for students to imbibe without straying too far from campus. On a typical night between 100 and 300 students came to the Rock Bottom Lounge.

A typical weekly schedule of events at the Rock Bottom Lounge in 1980 was football on Monday night, talent night on Tuesday, live jazz on Wednesday and special events on Thursday. Friday night was devoted to country and western music, and Saturday was disco night. Music in the lounge was a reflection of the time and tastes of the students. By the mid-1980s the Friday-night disco party was replaced by a more modern "nightclub" night with "new wave" music. Known as "Club RBL," the weekly event was modeled after "new music" clubs in Dallas like Club Clearview and Club Da-Da.

The Rock Bottom Lounge also featured stand-up comedy, hosting local performers as well as nationally known comics such as Elaine Boosler, who appeared in the lounge in 1988. Students were also invited to tell their favorite jokes at Amateur Comedy Night, which replaced talent night by the mid-1980s. Other events, such as a plays, Q&A sessions and a reading series were held in the lounge as well. Football Coach Corky Nelson held a series of lectures, called "Corky's Clinic," on the finer points of football starting in 1984. Although these lectures were primarily aimed at "women who don't know anything about football," men were invited as well.

Texas raised the legal drinking age to 21 in 1986, greatly affecting the Rock Bottom Lounge. Campus administrators decided to continue serving alcohol in the pub while putting security measures, such as wristbands and hand stamps, in place to limit underage drinking. The Rock Bottom Lounge was closed in the early 1990s as concern increased about college students and drinking. Gone but not forgotten, many former students still have fond memories of drinking, dining and listening to music at the club.

A cowboy and a woman with a pumpkin mask enjoy the 1979 Halloween party at the Rock Bottom Lounge. *From the University Photography Collection (U0458).*

Three revelers, one wearing a skeleton mask, stand outside the Rock Bottom Lounge during the 1979 Halloween party. *From the University Photography Collection (U0458).*

The glowing neon sign of the Rock Bottom Lounge photographed during a Halloween Party, 1979. *From the University Photography Collection (U0458).*

Two revelers enjoy the Halloween party at the Rock Bottom Lounge, 1979. *From the University Photography Collection (U0458).*

A group of costumed friends at the 1979 Halloween party held at the Rock Bottom Lounge. *From the University Photography Collection (U0458).*

The Man Who Made the Accordion Cool

Of all the talented musicians to have graduated from UNT, one stands out for his contribution to the art of accordion playing and for his impact on the Denton music community. Carl Finch started the band Brave Combo in 1979, the same year he completed his M.F.A. at North Texas. A mainstay of the Texas music scene today, Brave Combo's sound is often described as "polka" or "world music" and combines influences ranging from Polish American polka to zydeco.

In the late 1970s, however, the sounds of polka music was anything but cool. So what inspired this talented musician to pick up an accordion? In a book commissioned by the Special Collections department of the UNT Libraries, Finch explains it like this:

Accordion music, polka in particular, was the dumbest music one could listen to according to the people who controlled mainstream thought, and, certainly, no one could be both hip and appreciate the accordion at the same time. So I decided that if one had to be square to like accordions then squareness had to be embraced; being square had to be okay. The love of accordion music had to be seriously real or the band would only live in novelty kitsch-land, and that was not where the band wanted to be. This was hard-core for us; never ever a joke. The deep, unexplainable joy that music evokes, which often comes from laughing at oneself, had to flourish. Nothing was sacred as everything was sacred. There was no hip and there was no square. That's what we discovered, the truth, which was bigger than the music, but totally about the music.

Since their list of accolades and recognition continues to grow, there is no question that Finch and Brave Combo have succeeded in making the accordion cool. The band won a Grammy Award in 1999 for their album *Polkasonic* and another Grammy Award in 2004 for their album Let's Kiss. They made a cameo appearance in David Byrne's cult classic film *True Stories*, recorded original songs for the television show *Futurama* and appeared as animated characters on *The Simpsons*.

For over thirty five years, Finch and Brave Combo have made an incredible musical journey, which has taken them around the world, yet they have maintained their roots in Denton and continue to support the local music community. Brave Combo maintains a music studio in Denton on the burgeoning "Music Row" section of North Locust Street near the Courthouse Square.

To celebrate the band's 35th anniversary, the Special Collections department commissioned the creation of a unique artist's book made from one of Carl Finch's accordions. Artists' books are unique works of art that incorporate the structure or concept of a book in their form. The Brave Combo Accordion Book is a playful take on a traditional folding book structure commonly known as an "accordion book" but using an actual accordion. With this

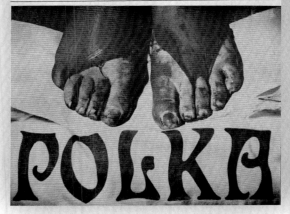

BRAVE COMBO   MUSIC FOR SQUARES

POLKA

Cover of Brave Combo's 1981 LP *Music for Squares. From the
private collection of Morgan Gieringer.*

Finch (*standing left*) and Barnes (*standing right*) entertaining students outside of the third union
building, 1985. *From the University Photography Collection (U0458).*

Photograph of Brave Combo members from a photo shoot for *North Texan* magazine. *Left to
right:* Lyle Atkinson, Carl Finch, Tim Walsh and Dave Cameron, 1980. *From the University
Photography Collection (U0458).*

work, the UNT Libraries have preserved an important piece of Brave Combo history while also contributing a new piece to an existing collection of artists' books.

The Brave Combo Accordion Book was created by book artists Peter and Donna Thomas using text, photographs and an accordion supplied by the band. When opened, the interior of the accordion displays "pages" of the book. One side contains hand-tinted photographs of Brave Combo, and the other side contains a narrative titled "The Story of Brave Combo," authored by Finch. Because the bellows of the accordion were removed in the creation of the book it no longer makes music, but it serves as a lasting homage to the man who made the accordion cool.

Finch and Barnes entertaining students outside of the third union building, 1985. *From the University Photography Collection (U0458).*

Thomas, Peter, Donna Thomas and Carl Finch. *Brave Combo Accordion Book.* 2014 (N7433.4.T56 B73 2014). This original artist's book was created for the Special Collections department of the UNT Libraries. The accordion housing the book belonged to Finch, the founder of Brave Combo.

Finch and Barnes entertaining students outside of the third union building, 1985. *From the University Photography Collection (U0458).*

"Miracle on Ice" Inspires Hockey Club

The 1980 Winter Olympic Games in Lake Placid, New York, are remembered as an exciting year for ice-hockey fans. It was there that the US hockey team won an upset victory over the Soviet Union, clinching the win in the final few seconds of the game in what came to be called "the Miracle on Ice." This historic match inspired a generation of hockey fans as well as one determined professor at North Texas.

"We've been told it can't be done," said Will Powers, a faculty member in the Department of Speech and Drama at North Texas. "We've been told the people in Denton are too closed-minded. They're too conservative. They're too used to the traditional. But we don't buy it—so far." It was Powers' dream to start a collegiate hockey club at UNT, and capitalizing on the excitement generated by the "Miracle on Ice," he was able to recruit student players and organize the first hockey club at North Texas in 1981. To qualify as a team member, a player had to be a student enrolled in at least six hours of college classes and be between the ages of 17 and 27.

Powers was an avid hockey fan. Prior to coaching the Hockey Club of North Texas, he had served as a sports psychology consultant to the Fort Worth Texans of the Central Hockey League.

Powers organized a club of supporters in the Denton area to support his cause even before the Hockey Club of North Texas had played their first game. These boosters, known as the "Hockey Heroes," received membership cards and newsletters updating them on the club's progress. The first issue of *Hockey Hero News*, issued in June 1981 to almost 200 subscribers, announced that North Texas had been accepted as a member of the Southwestern Collegiate Hockey Conference and would have a twenty-game schedule in the 1981–1982 season.

A July 1981 article in the *Denton Record-Chronicle* posed an important question to Powers: can a hockey team survive in a town without an ice rink? The team practiced at the Richardson Ice Palace, one of only three ice rinks in the Dallas–Fort Worth area large enough for a hockey game, and the team played its home games at the Will Rogers Coliseum in Fort Worth. With a healthy dose of optimism Powers replied, "We hope to have an ice rink here in Denton by this time next year."

In their first season the Hockey Club of North Texas played against well-established teams from the University of Texas at Austin, Louisiana State University, Tulane University and Southern Methodist University. The conference final was a surprise almost as big as the "Miracle on Ice" in 1980: the Hockey Club North Texas club finished their first season as conference champions.

Unfortunately the challenges facing the club were too strong to overcome. Despite the enthusiasm of the players and the coach, the Hockey Club ceased after one exciting year. The lack of a local ice rink and the cost of ice time were major factors in the short life of this club.

Poster advertising the Hockey Club's competition schedule for the 1981–82 season. *From the Hockey Club of North Texas Collection (U0479).*

Hockey Club recruitment poster distributed on campus in 1981. The poster advertises that attendees can "See U.S. Olympic Team Highlights Film." *From the Hockey Club of North Texas Collection (U0479).*

An article from *Hockey Hero News*, June 23, 1981. *From the Hockey Club of North Texas Collection (U0479).*

Article from the *North Texas Daily*, April 16, 1981.

The UNT University Archive is now home to artifacts from the hockey club's memorable year, donated by Powers in 2013. These include a scrapbook of hockey club memorabilia, a poster advertising the 1981–1982 Southwestern Collegiate Hockey Conference, news clippings documenting the club's formation and a t-shirt emblazoned with the logo of the Hockey Club of North Texas.

Pages from the scrapbook kept by Powers to document the activities of the Hockey Club. *From the Hockey Club of North Texas Collection (U0479).*

Hockey Hero booster club membership card. *From the Hockey Club of North Texas Collection (U0479).*

Hockey Club of North Texas t-shirt. *From the Hockey Club of North Texas Collection (U0479).*

The Mean, the Green, the . . . Armadillos?

These days, when UNT students want to cheer on the Mean Green, they attend a game at the new Apogee Stadium, the centerpiece of the Mean Green Athletic Village. But 24 years ago, there were *two* football teams on campus fighting for the students' attention. The fictional Texas State University Armadillos competed for attention on and off field, boasting a star-studded roster of actors and comedians including Scott Bakula, Robert Loggia, Jason Bateman, Kathy Ireland and Sinbad.

The UNT campus and its football field served as backdrop for the 1991 comedy film *Necessary Roughness*. In the movie, the Texas State Armadillos follow a string of successful seasons with a host of NCAA violations. The scandal forces them to forfeit their previous victories and clean house, leaving them with no coaches and only a single remaining player. Facing new restrictions and an unsupportive administration, their only hope is to hold try-outs and cobble together a 17-man team for iron-man football. Scott Bakula joins the team as Paul Blake, a 34-year-old quarterback whose bright future playing college ball was cut short when his father died. To be eligible to play ball, Blake has to enroll in college full time and keep his grades up or get cut from the team.

The basic plot was inspired by "Ponygate," the massive football scandal involving Southern Methodist University in the late 1980s. The NCAA invoked the "death penalty" due to continued violations, forcing SMU to cancel their entire 1987 football program.

Filming took place on campus from April 17 through June 1, 1991. During filming, UNT students had multiple opportunities to be extras both on and off the field. For the use of its facilities, the University was compensated $65,000. As an added bonus, 24 students studying radio, television and film gained valuable filming experience working with Paramount Pictures staff as production assistants during filming.

This wasn't the first time the UNT campus was featured in a major film. During the spring of 1984, Paramount Pictures filmed parts of *The Jesse Owens Story* at North Texas. The made-for-TV movie chronicles Owen's life and his rise to fame as a record-setting Olympic track-and-field star and one of the greatest modern American athletes. Filming took place at Fouts Field because producers were looking for a location that resembled a stadium at a Big Ten Conference school in the 1930's, though Texas' moderate climate was taken into consideration as well.

Luckily the students chosen as extras for *Necessary Roughness* were allowed to keep their own haircuts, but in order to be an extra for *The Jesse Owens Story*, students were given complimentary Marine-style crewcuts reminiscent of the 1930's!

Lisa Brown, a staff member of the UNT Libraries, attended UNT the year they were filming *Necessary Roughness* and recalls fondly what it was like to run into celebrities on your way to class. "I watched a scene being

Chancellor Alfred F. Hurley (*right*) poses with Héctor Elizondo (left), who played Coach Ed Gennero. *From the University Photography Collection (U0458).*

Cast members joke with one another in between takes. *Left to right:* Dick Butkus, Scott Bakula and Sinbad. *From the University Photography Collection (U0458).*

Dueling mascots! Eppy the Eagle (North Texas' mascot between 1983 and 1995) faces off against Rowdy, mascot for the fictional Fighting Armadillos. *From the University Photography Collection (U0458).*

World heavyweight champion Evander Holyfield enjoys a refreshing beverage off camera. *From the University Photography Collection (U0458).*

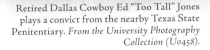

Retired Dallas Cowboy Ed "Too Tall" Jones plays a convict from the nearby Texas State Penitentiary. *From the University Photography Collection (U0458).*

Coach Ed "Straight Arrow" Gennero (Elizondo) is brought on to ensure a scandal-free season, but he has his work cut out for him. *From the University Photography Collection (U0458).*

A cameraman poses during the filming of *The Jesse Owens Story*, also filmed at Fouts Field. *From the University Photography Collection (U0458).*

filmed with Scott Bakula and Sinbad in front of the Library," she said. "There was a dolly set along the Library Mall for a tracking shot, and I remember thinking Scott Bakula was a lot cuter in person!"

In addition to movie stars, *Necessary Roughness* also features a slew of famous athletes during a scrimmage scene where the Armadillos face off against convicts from the Texas State Penitentiary. Jerry Rice, Dick Butkus, Herschel Walker, Tony Dorsett and championship boxer Evander Holyfield give the Fighting Armadillos a run for their money.

Fans of the sitcom *Arrested Development* will appreciate watching Bateman in his second earliest film role (his breakthrough role was four years prior, in *Teen Wolf Too*). How did Bateman enjoy his time in Denton? Bateman, playing fullback, said in an interview with yearbook staff that he liked Denton and had visited before for his "girlfriend's step-sister's wedding."

The majority of the film was shot on the UNT campus, but other locations around the Dallas–Fort Worth area got their moment in the spotlight. The film's famous fight scene, where Armadillo players squared off against the University of Texas Colts, was shot at Billy Bob's nightclub in Fort Worth. Watch the movie and see if you recognize any of your favorite places on campus, or see just how much campus has changed in the twenty-four years since the movie was shot.

Cast members relax off camera while filming the scrimmage scene. *Left to right*: Butkus, Bakula and Sinbad. *From the University Photography Collection (U0458)*.

The film crew needed plenty of shade to film outdoors in the Texas summer heat. In fact, this is one of the only photos where the production crew isn't shirtless! *From the University Photography Collection (U0458)*.

Lucy Draper (Kathy Ireland) is recruited from the women's soccer team as a kicker. *From the University Photography Collection (U0458)*.

The cast poses for publicity shots between takes. *Left to right*: Louis Mandylor, Bakula and Sinbad. *From the University Photography Collection (U0458)*.

UNT students who participated as extras were treated to hot dogs, sodas and memorabilia with the fictitious Texas State University insignia. *From the University Artifacts Collection (U0493)*.

Driving into the Future

In 1990 UNT kicked off a full year of celebration to mark the university's 100th anniversary. The Centennial Extravaganza, a performance which took place at Fouts Field in October, was the focus of many student's attention. Featuring a cast of hundreds of actors, the Extravaganza showcased the history of UNT through an original stage production featuring music composed by students and faculty in the School of Music. Students working under the direction of a professional costume designer produced 2,575 costumes representing different periods in the university's history.

There were other events as well. One of the more unique commemorations of the centennial was by the Department of Industrial Technology whose students participated in the design and construction of a solar car. The car, named *Centennial*, took part is an eleven-day race of solar cars sponsored by General Motors called Sunrayce USA. Fitting for an institution with a mascot named Scrappy, the UNT team went up against 32 other teams with the fewest team members and the least expensive car ($70,000) of any other tem. (For comparison, the University of Michigan team had an $800,000 car.) Faculty advisors John Dobson and Therrill Valentine and team leader Lee Palmer supervised a ten-member student team in two years of design and building, including tests in the wind tunnel at Texas A&M, to create UNT's solar car. They submitted a proposal to the race organizers, and Palmer reported that one of them, an employee of the US Department of Energy, said that parts of UNT's proposal went over his head. UNT's submission was one of only two from Texas and one of only three chosen from a university without an engineering school.

The car was sixteen feet long, with three wheels and one seat. The vehicle was only 34½ inches tall, tapering to just a few inches in the rear, and had only a three-inch ground clearance. The lightest car in the race (just 377 pounds), it held a one horse-power engine yet still reached speeds of 23 miles per hour. UNT's team placed twelfth in the qualifying race, with a time of 11 hours and 38 minutes at the Daytona Speedway in Florida.

During the race, life for the team members was not easy. Their day started at 5 a.m., when they used the early-morning sun to charge the batteries for a couple of hours. They then raced for nine hours and began charging the batteries again. Members of the team took 4½-hour shifts driving the car. There was only a small space for the driver and no air conditioning, so the driver often worked in temperatures reaching 105 degrees. The car's most common problem during the race was flat tires, which happened seven times. Furthermore, the team was unable to race for two days due to frequent rain, which had an impact on the placement of the team. The Centennial finished the race in 18th place.

The solar car's design team with the skeleton of the car during construction. *From the University Photography Collection (U0458).*

Actors performing an original musical piece at the Centennial Extravaganza. *From the University Photography Collection (U0458).*

Students assisting in costume design for the Centennial Extravaganza. *From the University Photography Collection (U0458).*

The UNT solar car was an early foray into a university-wide commitment to sustainability. The College of Engineering operates the Zero Energy Research Lab, the only facility in Texas for testing net-zero energy consumption. Today UNT boasts four LEED-certified buildings on campus, a robust recycling program and one of the only all-vegan campus dining halls in the country. The university has also been recognized by the NCAA for having "a greener game day" because of the three wind turbines, installed in 2011 and operating since 2012, which help supply energy to Apogee Stadium. In fact, UNT gets almost half of its energy from renewable sources.

The UNT solar car was named Centennial in honor of the university's 100th anniversary. This profile of the car shows how low to the ground it stood. *From the University Photography Collection (U0458).*

Commemorative medals given to attendees at the 1990 Centennial Extravaganza. *From the University Photography Collection (U0458).*

The cars raced on active roadways. General Motors provided two regular cars to each team to move the other team members and provide technical support during the race. *From the University Photography Collection (U0458).*

The solar car team poses with UNT's car during a repair stop along the side of the road. The race was held in July 1990. John Dobson, center, was one of the team's faculty advisors. *From the University Photography Collection (U0458).*